STRESS TEST

STRESS TEST

THOMAS WHITEMAN PH.D. & RANDY PETERSEN

A Quick Guide to Finding and Improving Your Stress Quotient

PIÑON PRESS

P.O. Box 35007, Colorado Springs, Colorado 80935

OUR GUARANTEE TO YOU

We believe so strongly in the message of our books that we are making this quality guarantee to you. If for any reason you are disappointed with the content of this book, return the title page to us with your name and address and we will refund to you the list price of the book. To help us serve you better, please briefly describe why you were disappointed. Mail your refund request to: Piñon Press, P.O. Box 35002, Colorado Springs, CO 80935.

Library of Congress Catalog Card Number: 99-047780
ISBN 1-57683-035-7

Cover illustration by Theo Rudnak/The Stock Illustration Source, Inc.
Cover Design by Dan Jamison
Creative Team: Brad Lewis, Darla Hightower, Tim Howard

Some of the anecdotal illustrations in this book are true to life and are included with the permission of the persons involved. We have changed the names and identifying details of the persons involved. All other illustrations are composites of real situations, and any resemblance to people living or dead is coincidental.

This publication is designed to provide accurate and authoritative information in regard to the subject matter covered. It is sold with the understanding that the author and the publisher are not engaged in rendering legal, accounting, or other professional service. If legal advice or other expert assistance is required, the services of a competent professional person should be sought. *From a Declaration of Principles jointly adopted by a Committee of the American Bar Association and a Committee of Publishers.*

Unless otherwise identified, all Scripture quotations in this publication are taken from the *HOLY BIBLE: NEW INTERNATIONAL VERSION* © (NIV®). Copyright © 1973, 1978, 1984 by International Bible Society. Used by permission of Zondervan Publishing House. All rights reserved. Other versions used include: the *Revised Standard Version Bible* (RSV), copyright © 1946, 1952, 1971 by the Division of Christian Education of the National Council of the Churches of Christ in the USA, used by permission, all rights reserved.

Whiteman, Tom.
    Stress Test: a quick guide to finding and improving your stress quotient / Thomas Whiteman and Randy Petersen.
        p.   cm.
    ISBN 1-57683-035-7
    1. Stress (Psychology). 2. Stress management. 3. Stress management—Religious aspects—Christianity. I. Petersen, Randy. II. Title.

BF575.S75 W47 2000
155.9'042—dc21   99-047780

Printed in the United States of America

1 2 3 4 5 6 7 8 9 10/05 04 03 02 01 00 99

Contents

Taking the Test

PART ONE

LIFE is stressful. Unless you've managed to get away from it all, retiring to some idyllic island, you're surely experiencing stress on a regular basis. And even on that island you might begin to worry about something—say, coconuts falling on your head. There's always something.

In a way, you need stress. When you finally get rid of all the stress in your life, you'll be dead. Our daily challenges keep us going. Some people say they thrive on stress. Without a deadline to meet, some nearly impossible task to perform, or a major life drama unfolding—they get bored. When things are too quiet, they worry about what's *not* happening and why. Some people even stir things up at home or at work as part of an unconscious need for excitement.

Yet others need that quiet existence. Under pressure, they choke—sweaty palms, a racing heart, stammered words, random thoughts. They just can't handle stress. Such people become gardeners, not Wall Street brokers.

In the last generation, the world has learned a great deal about the negative effects of stress. High stress can do a number on your heart, raising your blood pressure. It can put a damper on your immune system, making you susceptible to all sorts of diseases.

But stress comes in different forms, from different sources, and people deal with it in different ways.

A woman may be handling a high-stress job day-in, day-out, with vibrant energy—but then she gets a divorce and she falls apart from the stress of that event. A brother and sister may both experience the tragic death of their father, but the sister gets over it quickly while the brother doesn't.

As you try to gauge the stress in your life and its impact, it's not just a question of *how much stress.* You need to consider whether it's a sudden event or an ongoing environment. You need to add up all the other stress in your life. And you need to consider how ready you are to roll with it. Can you accept it and move on, or do you make things worse by worrying or by diving into some self-destructive habit?

People like stress tests. They'll see a list of questions in a magazine and they'll pull out a Bic and circle the appropriate answers. When they total their responses, they check their score against the chart and learn that they have a lot of stress ("Aha," they say, "I was right! I *am* stressed!"), or maybe a medium amount ("Hmm. It's not as bad as I thought . . . "). If they have little stress, they're probably not taking the test.

These tests are fun, but they're just warning flags. They tend to confirm what you already know. You get a numerical score that quantifies your stress. Presumably, you can compare your number with everyone on your block to figure out where you fit in the stress standings. Are you better or worse off than your neurotic neighbor?

But as we've seen, people handle stress differently. And stress comes in different forms, from different sources. To get a realistic stress map, you need to evaluate several factors. You need more than a number, you need a whole equation.

You probably took an IQ test as a child, giving you a number—your Intelligence Quotient—that defined how smart you were (or so you presumed). For a few generations in our culture, this number reigned supreme—the commonly accepted measure of a person's mental ability. But more recently, researchers have discovered different types of intelligence, as many as seven of them—linear, verbal, spatial, creative, and so forth. But you knew that, didn't you? Johnny couldn't read well, but he could draw anyone or anything. Sally couldn't remember the multiplication tables, but she seemed to sense whenever you were upset. Maybe you had trouble with names and dates in history class, but you could sure pack a car trunk. Different measures are required for different abilities. And that's the beauty of more recent research into IQ testing. As many as a dozen different subtest scores are analyzed in order to give you feedback on specific strengths and weaknesses in your cognitive functioning. Those subtest scores, and the profile they create, are far more important than the one-dimensional IQ number.

Recently, one psychologist coined the term *Emotional Intelligence* to explain people's varying abilities to cope with their emotions. You need more than an IQ test, he theorizes. You need an EQ test. Your Emotional Quotient, he says, is a greater predictor of success in life than your IQ. That concept brings us even closer to our thoughts on the Stress Quotient.

As we've researched the issue of stress, we've realized that this area is similar to IQ and EQ. You need an SQ, a Stress Quotient, to help you understand your stress level and why you might faint at challenges other people thrive on. But, as with intelligence, you need more than a score, you need a map. You need a diagnostic snapshot of the different kinds of stress you're facing and how you cope with them.

The Factors

First, we need to look at the differences between stress events and stress environments. *Stress events* are those traumatic occurrences that affect us deeply—the death of a loved one, a divorce, an accident, a natural disaster, the loss of a job, a financial loss, a major illness. And stress events aren't only negative. A new job, a financial investment, or moving to a new location can be positive events, but they can also be major stressors. These events sometimes occur suddenly. We can't prepare for them, and we can't avoid them.

Our *stress environments* are ongoing. Your family, your job, your neighborhood—these surroundings can pound you regularly with stress. Can you make these environments less stressful? Yes, but it's not easy. You can improve a family situation with communication or therapy. You could quit your job or move to a new neighborhood (though those actions might produce more stress).

But there are still some people who live and work in high-stress environments—yet when terrible things happen to them, they stay healthy and happy. Others seem to have it better, yet they're all stressed out. What gives?

Two other factors enter the equation: stress aggravators and stress fitness. *Stress aggravators* occur when people worry about everything, making the situation seem worse than it is. Or they deal with stress by plunging into self-destructive habits—such as gambling or drinking heavily—and these activities just make their lives more stressful. The problem with aggravators is that stress triggers these behaviors, and they result in greater stress. They can be curbed, but only with an aggressive commitment to behavior change.

Stress fitness is the area that usually gets most of the attention in stress-management books. If you eat right, sleep well, and exercise enough, you can strengthen your body against the damage of stress. If you meditate, pray, and draw strength from God and your relationships, you can fortify your soul. Most of us could stand to improve in at least one of these areas.

The Equation

Putting together these four factors—Stress Events (SV), Stress Environment (SN), Aggravators (A), and Fitness (F)—we get this equation:

$$\frac{(SV + SN) \times A}{F} = SQ$$

Your Stress Quotient(SQ) combines your Stress Events and Environment, multiplies them by your Aggravators, and divides by your Fitness. That's the theory. While you haven't plugged in any numbers yet, think about the relationships within this equation. If you add a one-time stressful event to your ongoing stressful environment, you have a pile of stress—maybe a big pile, maybe not. But if you worry, gamble, get drunk, or do anything else to aggravate the situation, that pile of stress gets doubled or tripled in size. You just make everything worse. On the other hand, if you practice good stress fitness—eating, sleeping, exercising, and thinking properly—you can cut your stress pile down significantly.

Changing Your Score

How can you change your Stress Quotient? If you are overstressed, what can you do about it? Mathematically, there are four ways to lower your SQ, and they correspond to four strategies for reducing stress. You could lessen your Stress Events, Stress Environments, or Aggravators, or you could improve your Fitness.

Frankly, in the first area, Stress Events, you don't have much control. Stressful things will happen to you from time to time. The good news is that over time you naturally recover from these events, unless you delay your recovery with a high-stress environment or aggravators. The bad news is that you never know when another stress event will strike. So it doesn't make a lot of sense to try reducing the stress events in your life. They will happen and you will naturally recover. Instead, work on improving the other three areas of the equation—Stress Environment, Aggravators, and Fitness.

The following test asks you to evaluate your own stress situation in all four areas. It also breaks down environmental stress into three different environments. After you take the test, a strategy for stress reduction should emerge.

The test is somewhat scientific in that we tested it with various groups to make sure the different elements balanced properly. But it is still a self-test, completely subjective. You are recording how you feel about certain things. We're not taking objective measurements of your pulse or blood pressure. The test relies on your fair and honest appraisal of the stress factors in your life.

But don't let the test stress you out. Seriously, it won't matter to anyone else whether you score high or low. It's only meant to give you feedback on what *you* reported. The test is for your benefit, to analyze the interplay of stress factors in your own life and to point out some ways to improve your stress situation.

When you look back over your answers, this test will give you much more than a number. It will give you a map. And that map will give you a plan, an agenda for change.

NOTE: You'll want to take the test again in the future, so it's best to make photocopies of these test pages and write on those papers. In fact, having your answers on a separate sheet will make it easier to refer to the test as you read the rest of the book. We grant permission for you to photocopy the test for yourself and those in your immediate household. If you want your friends to take the test, buy them the book.

We also have the test on a CD-ROM version. It will automatically score and graph your results if you take the test on your computer. The CD is available for a small shipping and handling fee by calling 1-800-882-2799. Or you may visit our Web site at www.lifecounseling.org.

STRESS QUOTIENT TEST

Please complete the following personal information:

Male___ Female___ Single___ Married___

Optional: ethnic background _____

Age Range: 6-21 22-30 31-40 41-50 Over 50

WORK STRESS

Answer the following questions as they relate to your job, or the work that you do. If you are a full-time student who is not working, substitute "school" for work.

1. On a scale from one to five, how would you rate the amount of stress you experience in the workplace?

1	2	3	4	5
Slight		Moderate		Severe

2. How much change do you experience in the workplace, such as instability, fluctuating job requirements, or an erratic boss?

1	2	3	4	5
Slight		Moderate		Severe

3. How vulnerable do you feel in the workplace, such as fearing a layoff, feeling unsafe, or in some other way threatened?

1	2	3	4	5
Slight		Moderate		Severe

4. Do you sense a lack of control on your job, such as an inability to effect change or inability to have an impact on the decisions that are made?

1	2	3	4	5
Slight		Moderate		Severe

5. Do you have a heavy workload and find that you can't complete tasks on schedule?

1	2	3	4	5
Slight		Moderate		Severe

6. How poor is the communication in your workplace, such as vague goals and objectives, or unclear expectations?

1	2	3	4	5
Slight		Moderate		Severe

7. How responsible are you for the well-being and/or the job performance of others?

1	2	3	4	5
A Little		Moderate		A Lot

8. Do you find your coworkers difficult to work with?

1	2	3	4	5
Slight		Moderate		Severe

Add your scores for items 1-8 and record the total here:

Work Stress Score: _____
(Enter here and on page 24)

RELATIONAL STRESS

Answer the following questions as they relate to your primary relationship. Primary relationships can be your spouse, your child or children, your parent or parents, your roommate, your boyfriend or girlfriend—whomever you interact with on a most significant level.

9. How much stress do you experience in your primary relationship?

1	2	3	4	5
Not at all	Slight	Moderate	Strong	Severe

10. How unstable do you feel in your relationship, such as the other person being unpredictable, moody, or volatile?

1	2	3	4	5
Not at all	Slight	Moderate	Strong	Severe

11. How threatened do you feel that your primary relationship could experience a breakup?

1	2	3	4	5
Not at all	Slight	Moderate	Strong	Severe

12. How valued or understood do you feel in your relationship?

1	2	3	4	5
Highly Valued	Usually Valued	Moderately Valued	Slightly Valued	Not Valued

13. Has your primary relationship become boring or unsatisfying?

1	2	3	4	5
Not at all	Slight	Moderate	Strong	Severe

14. How difficult is the communication in your primary relationship?

1	2	3	4	5
Not at all	Slight	Moderate	Strong	Severe

15. How much conflict do you experience in your primary relationship?

1	2	3	4	5
Not at all	Slight	Moderate	Strong	Severe

16. How much stress do you experience in your secondary relationships, such as with a close friend or a family member?

1	2	3	4	5
Not at all	Slight	Moderate	Strong	Severe

Add your scores for items 9-16 and record the total here:

Relational Stress Score:_____
(Enter here and on page 24)

17. How secure, or confident, do you feel in your abilities?

1	2	3	4	5
Highly Secure	Secure	Neutral	Insecure	Very Insecure

18. How satisfied are you with your life right now?

1	2	3	4	5
Very Satisfied	Usually Satisfied	Moderately Satisfied	Unsatisfied	Very Unsatisfied

19. Do you have unresolved issues from your past or family of origin which affect you today?

1	2	3	4	5
Very slight		Some issues		Numerous unresolved issues

20. Are you concerned about the future?

1	2	3	4	5
Very slight		Moderately		Seriously concerned

21. How unsafe do you feel in your neighborhood?

1	2	3	4	5
Slight		Moderate		Severe

22. How difficult are traffic, congestion, and transportation problems for you in your community?

1	2	3	4	5
Slight		Moderate		Severe

23. How isolated do you feel in your neighborhood?

1	2	3	4	5
Slight		Moderate		Severe

24. How unpleasant are your neighbors or neighborhood?

1	2	3	4	5
Slight		Moderate		Severe

Add your scores for items 17-24 and record the total here:

Personal and Community Stress Score:_____
(Enter here and on page 24)

25. Have you experienced a major stress event in the last two years? A major event would be comparable to a death in the immediate family, divorce, job loss, a new marriage, or diagnosis of a major illness.

0	10	20	30
No	Yes, but it was more than a year ago	Yes, but it was more than three months ago	Yes, within the last three months

26. Have you experienced one or more moderate stress events in the last month? A moderate stress event would be comparable to a relationship conflict, a parent/child conflict, a significant change in financial or job status, a major project or assignment, or a conflict within your primary social circle.

0	5	10	15
No	Yes, but it was mild	Yes	Yes, and it hit me especially hard

27. Of the *major* stressors, have you experienced more than one in the last two years?

0	10	20
No	Yes, 2	Yes, 3 or more

28. Of the *moderate* stressors, have you experienced more than one in the last month?

0	10	20
No	Yes, 2	Yes, 3 or more

Add your scores for items 25-28 and record the total here:

Stress Event Score: _____
(Enter here and on page 24)

29. Do you tend to make "mountains out of molehills," taking a stressful event and magnifying it, or obsessing about the event?

0	1	2	3	4	5
No	Very slight		Much of the time		I do that all the time

30. Do you tend to be your own worst enemy by taking an event and beating yourself up over it, blaming yourself or berating yourself over that event?

0	1	2	3	4	5
No	Very slight		Much of the time		I do that all the time

31. Do you put things off until the last minute?—procrastinating to the point of making projects worse than they need to be?

0	1	2	3	4	5
No	Very slight		Much of the time		I do that all the time

32. Do you tend to take on too much responsibility, saying "yes" to too many things, only to find yourself feeling overwhelmed?

0	1	2	3	4	5
No	Very slight		Much of the time		I do that all the time

33. Do you have compulsive or addictive behaviors such as smoking, overeating, drinking, gambling, or overspending?

0	1	2	3	4	5
No	Very slight		Much of the time		I do that all the time

34. Do you have a hard time forgiving others, holding on to grievances or your anger for longer than you should?

0	1	2	3	4	5
No	Very slight		Much of the time		I do that all the time

Add your scores for items 29-34 and then divide the total by 6. This will give you an average for the six items in this section. If your score is less than 1, please enter 1. (Use a caculator if this stresses you out!)

Total Score: _____

Divided by 6:

Aggravator Score: _____
(Enter here and on page 24)

NOTE: Your Aggravator Score cannot be less than 1.

35. Do you follow an exercise program each week?

0	1	2	3	4	5
Not at all	Very sporadic		Fairly regular		Diligent, at least 3 times a week

36. Are you good about eating nutritionally balanced and healthy meals? Do you also avoid smoking, excessive alcohol, or caffeine?

0	1	2	3	4	5
Not at all	Very slight		Much of the time		I do that all the time

37. Do you take regular breaks during the day in order to relax, especially during lunch? Do you also take a regular day off in order to relax or spend time with family and friends?

0	1	2	3	4	5
Not at all	Very slight		Much of the time		I do that all the time

38. Have you resolved issues or hurts from the past? Are you looking forward to a promising future?

0	1	2	3	4	5
Not at all	Very slight		Much of the time		I do that all the time

39. Do you have a strong faith, turning your worries over to God? Do you meditate or pray about things that are beyond your control?

0	1	2	3	4	5
Not at all	Very slight		Much of the time		I do that all the time

40. Have you set short- and long-term goals, updating them at appropriate intervals?

0	1	2	3	4	5
Not at all	Very slight		Much of the time		I do that all the time

41. Are you able to assert your feelings in appropriate ways?

0	1	2	3	4	5
Not at all	Very slight		Much of the time		I do that all the time

42. Do you place a high value on your primary relationship(s), and set aside time to work on improving it (them)?

0	1	2	3	4	5
Not at all	Very slight		Much of the time		I do that all the time

43. Do you have work, a hobby, or activities that give you a sense of meaning and purpose?

0	1	2	3	4	5
Not at all	Very slight		To a moderate level		I feel great about this area

44. Do you have a close network of friends or family that supports you emotionally and spiritually?

0	1	2	3	4	5
Not at all	Very slight		Pretty good		Wonderful network

Add your scores for items 35-44 and then divide the total by 10. If less than 1, please enter 1.

Total Score: _____

Divide by 10

Fitness Score: _____
(Enter here and on page 24)

NOTE: Your Fitness Score cannot be less than 1.

Finding your own SQ is a matter of following a mathematical formula that will give you insights into your own stress and clues as to what you might do to improve your score. If you have trouble with the math, we have a CD-ROM version of the test which will automatically score your test and print out your results. Call 1-800-882-2799 for a copy of the CD. You might also visit our Web site at www.lifecounseling.org.

SQ Formula:

$$\frac{(SV + SN) \times A}{F}$$

First step: Calculate your Stress Environment score by combining your Work Stress, Relational Stress, and Personal/Community Stress scores.

Work Stress   _____

Relational Stress   + _____

Personal/Community Stress   + _____

Stress Environment (SN) (Total) _____

Second step: Add your Stress Environment (SN) score to your Stress Event (SV) score. Then multiply that number by your Aggravators (A) score. (Remember: your Aggravators score is an average. It cannot be greater than 5. If your Aggravators score is less than 1, just enter 1.)

(SN _____ + SV_____ = _____) x A_____ = _____

Third step: Now you just have to divide by your Fitness (F) score. Once again, remember that this is an average score, and shouldn't exceed 5. (If your Fitness score is less than 1, just enter 1.)

$$\frac{(SV + SN) \times A}{F} = \underline{\hspace{2cm}} = SQ \underline{\hspace{2cm}}$$

Fourth step: Identify your problem areas. Look at each score within the formula and identify the scores you need to improve. Each part of the formula is more important than your overall score, so pay particular attention to any scores which seem high.

A closer look: Look for the questions where you scored a 4 or a 5 as a clue to areas you need to improve. On the Fitness side, examine areas where you scored 1 or 2. Keep in mind that *you will get the best results from working on your Aggravator score and your Fitness score.*

We've administered this test to several groups and compiled the norms that you'll see soon. But we're always working to improve it, so we'd be interested in assembling test results from the readers of this book. If you'd make a copy of your scoresheet and send it to us, we can include you in our new data. (And relax—your anonymity is assured.) Or you can always take the latest edition of the test online at our Web site. There, you will find updated norms, new product information, and you can e-mail us your results and comments.

To contact us:
Life Counseling Services
Attn: Tom Whiteman
63 Chestnut Rd.
Paoli, PA 19301
FAX: 610-644-4066
Phone: 1-800-882-2799
Web site: www.lifecounseling.org

Interpreting Your Score

"How did I do? Do I have too much stress? Is my score high or low?" That's what everyone wants to know.

That's understandable, but it misses the point. Because it's a self-test, your score is yours alone, and it only reflects what you told it. This is something like measuring a person's level of pain. One person will moan and whine over a paper cut while another practically gets run over by a tank and shrugs it off. Different people report their stress differently, so comparisons are difficult. We can tell you how your reporting compares to that of others, but the most important thing is for you to find ways to improve your own score.

For example, in the fitness section you're asked if you follow an exercise program each week. Joe may be very proud of the fact that he walks a flight of stairs to his office every day, instead of taking the elevator. He gives himself a 5 because, in his view, he's "diligent at least 3 times a week." Mary tries to run five miles on Mondays, Wednesdays, and Fridays, but she's been too busy on the last few Wednesdays. So she judges herself harshly and gives herself a 3 for being "fairly regular" in her exercise program. Any neutral observer would say that Mary is far more fit than Joe, but this test relies on their own opinions.

In the next question, Joe may think he eats "healthy meals" because once a week he has a salad slathered in bleu cheese dressing, while Mary has salads every day, but worries about the oil in her oil-and-vinegar dressing. Joe gives himself a 4 while Mary scrupulously claims only a 2.

Now, after a test full of answers like this, Joe has no business crowing about his lower stress score (and higher Fitness score). "Look, Mary, this proves I'm healthier than you are!" It doesn't prove anything like that. It merely shows that Mary is harder on herself. (Therefore, Mary will also have a higher Aggravator Score.)

Does that invalidate the test? Not at all. It just means that comparisons with others may be completely invalid. What is valid is the effort you exert to work toward improvement and looking at how you progress (by comparing your old scores with your new scores when you retake the test).

Comparative Norms

We analyzed the test results of approximately 500 people to develop the following comparative norms. We're guessing you'll compare your own scores with these norms. Just remember that the categories are general, so try to interpret your results as general guidelines, rather than as a prescription or diagnosis.

NORMS

	You're doing great! You should have written the book.*	These are average scores. Look at individual answers for clues about where to improve.	Your stress is above average. Improvement recommended.	Stress levels are very high. You need to take some action.
Work	8 - 14	15 - 19	20 - 25	26 +
Relational	8 - 12	13 - 17	18 - 24	25 +
Personal/ Community	8 - 11	12 - 16	17 - 23	24 +
Total Environment	24 - 39	40 - 55	56 - 72	73 +
Stress Events	0 - 12	13 - 30	31 - 45	46 +
Aggravators	1	1.1 - 2.4	2.5 - 3.0	3 +
TOTAL STRESS QUOTIENT	1 - 29*	30 - 70	71 - 99	100 +

Fitness Scores:	You're doing great! Keep up the good work.	Average scores— look for areas to improve.	You need to get to work.
	4.0 +	2.5 - 3.9	1 - 2.4

* If your scores are extremely low, that may be indicative of a very healthy, minimally stressed life. But there might be another explanation that's a little less noble. Every life should embrace a certain amount of stress— not so much to stress you out, but enough to make life interesting and challenging. Some who run away from any kind of stress at all may have very low scores. But they also may be missing many of the challenges that make life interesting and worthwhile. In a relationship, this may mean you avoid all conflict. While this keeps stress low, you may be missing out on the growth that occurs when people are stretched and challenged. At work, avoiding stress may hold you back from success and promotions given to those who are willing to tackle tough situations. Avoidance of all of life's challenges may also be indicative of depression. If you suspect that depression is the problem, you may want to contact your physician or a professional counselor for additional help.

What All This Means

If you look at each individual score and compare it to your total stress score, you'll get a good idea about how each area affects your overall stress. Clearly, the best way to improve your overall stress is to work on Aggravators and Fitness. While Work Stress, Relational Stress, and Stress Events had a correlation of about .4 to .5 with the total SQ (predicting about 40 percent to 50 percent of total stress), Fitness had a high correlation of .6 and Aggravators a very high .8! That means more than half of the people in stressful jobs or relationships can deal with the stress, keeping their total Stress Quotient to healthy levels. But only one in five people with serious Aggravators can compensate for those bad habits and get a healthy overall score.

Your Map

You already know you're stressed. That's why you're taking the test! What you need to know is where your stress is coming from, so the individual subtest scores (SN, SV, A, and F) are far more important than the overall score. Even if your subtest scores are average, you can still learn something from the individual questions!

Sean took the Stress Test at a conference where Tom was speaking, and her overall score was in the average range. She immediately challenged Tom on the test's validity. Her life was in turmoil because of a recent divorce, she said. How could she have an "average" amount of stress? A closer look revealed significantly high scores in Relational Stress and Stress Events—those reflect the divorce. But her Aggravator score was good and her Fitness score was very good. Though she was certainly hurting, and she could work on a few elements of Relational Stress, she wasn't compounding the stress of her divorce with Aggravators. In fact, she was regularly easing her stress levels with her great stress Fitness. As she healed from the pain of divorce, she'd be in great shape, stress-wise.

That Was Then, This Is Now

Plan to take the test again in three months or so. By that time you should address some of your problem areas, applying some of the stress-reduction suggestions we will talk about later. Compare your new score with your old score and see if you're improving. Keep taking the test at three- or four-month intervals and chart your progress.

If your score doesn't improve, don't despair. There are a few possible reasons for that.

Have you faced a new stress event? You may be making great strides in improving Fitness or reducing Aggravators, but your life has been rocked by a death in the family, the loss of a job, or some other catastrophe. These things are out of your control and they will naturally increase the stress in your life. You'll see this in your scoring by comparing the Stress Event (SV) levels. If the new SV score is much higher, obviously you're facing a tumultuous event and that's offsetting the improvements in other areas.

Has your environment become more stressful? Again, factors out of your control may be causing you stress. Has your business hit a busy season? Have your children reached an unruly age? Are your neighbors throwing dishes at each other? If your Stress Environment (SN) score has risen considerably from the previous test, it will erase the stress reduction you've accomplished in other areas. Try to pin down the source of the new stress and see what, if anything, you can do about it.

Are you compensating with different Aggravators? Counselors often talk about "cross-addiction." A person kicking drugs may smoke more cigarettes. And if you're reducing some of your stress-aggravating behaviors, other behaviors may arise to take their place. If the new behavior is more benign, this may not be a problem. Or it may just give you a new aggravator to target in the next six months.

Are you tackling a long-term problem? Smoking, for instance, is a stress aggravator. People turn to it when they feel stress, and it seems to calm them, but in the long run it hurts their health and increases their stress levels. So let's say you try to quit smoking to ease your stress. In the long run, that's a great idea, but this week, this month, maybe this whole year, your stress levels will skyrocket. So if you can handle this, do it—just don't expect lower stress in six months.

Are you more sensitive to problems now? You may actually be succeeding in reducing your stress levels, but you're just becoming more sensitive to stress. (Taking too many stress tests will do that to you.) So, in your self-reporting, you're becoming more like Mary, less like Joe. You demand more of yourself now. As a result, although your Fitness has improved, your score doesn't. You may have reduced some Aggravators, but you're more aware of others now. If this is the case, it's best to go back through the test with your old test in hand. On each question ask yourself, "Am I better in this area than I was before?"

Is stress reduction stressing you out? Some people get so sensitive to stress factors that stress reduction becomes a new stress aggravator. Does that make sense? They're constantly worrying about everything that happens to them: "Oh, no! I bet this will cause me stress!" Or they become such a pain in the neck to their family or coworkers that their environmental stress rises. (Of course that would never happen to you!) The key word is *relax!* Don't miss the forest for the trees. Don't tackle all the individual elements of stress reduction and miss the overall goal.

Break It Down

We've said it before and we'll say it again: Your final score is not the most important number here. Stress is a multifaceted thing, so you have to look at *all* your numbers—Stress Event (SV), Stress Environment (SN), Aggravators (A), and Fitness (F). See how they compare with one another.

First, compare the scores for your different environments. Do you have more stress at work, in your relationships, or in your personal/community life? That will tell you where you need to do some stress reduction. Obviously, the highest score signals your greatest area of stress. If all three scores are about the same, it will be harder to make a game plan. The "moderate" score is 24, so if you're in the 30s in all three areas, you're reporting high environmental stress everywhere. Quick! Take a vacation! But if they're all under 20, you're doing okay, as far as your stress environment goes.

In our testing, the work environment earned the highest stress scores for most people. That makes sense. Work is supposed to be stressful. That's why they have to pay you to do it. And you can get by in a high-stress job, as long as your other environments aren't adding significantly to your stress.

Now, look at your Stress Event score. This is more *descriptive* than *prescriptive*. That is, there's not a lot you can do about stress events, except allow yourself to heal. But if you feel especially stressed these days and you see a score of 40 or more in this category, that explains it. You're still reeling from your latest stress event. The maximum score here is 75 — for multiple major and moderate stress events within the last few months. If your score is up in that stratosphere, it's not your fault, but you'll need to do some serious stress management over the next several months. You can't hurry your healing, but you can cut yourself some slack in other areas of your life.

Next, compare your Aggravators score with your Fitness score. Which is higher? If it's the Aggravators, the net effect is that you're making your stress worse. If it's the Fitness, your good habits are easing your stress situation. The average score for each is 3. Ideally, your Aggravators should be under 3 and your Fitness over 3. If it's the other way around, you need some work on both.

You know the deodorant ad that says it's "body heat activated"? The protection supposedly turns on when you need it most. Well, stress aggravators and fitness work the same way. If the stress from your environment and events is low, aggravators don't hurt you that much. But when stress is high, aggravators make it higher. And that's exactly when the advantage of your stress fitness kicks in.

Your Personal Strategy

Your Aggravator and Fitness scores have the biggest effect on your overall score. They're also the two areas where you have the greatest control. Any work you do in these two areas will multiply the positive effects in your life and minimize the negatives.

Take a moment now to start formulating your strategy. Based on your environment numbers, which area(s) should you be working to improve? Do you need to reduce your aggravators or heighten your stress fitness or both? After analyzing your score, you should have one to three items on your stress management agenda.

Here's an example of how this works. Kim (not her real name) produced a scoresheet that looked like this:

Work Stress 19
Relational Stress 30
Personal/Community Stress 17
Stress Environment (SN) Total 66
Stress Events (SV) 25
Aggravators (A) 3.3
Fitness (F) 2.4

$$\frac{[\text{SN } (66) + \text{SV } (25)] \times A\ (3.3)}{F\ (2.4)} = 125$$

Her final score of 125 is significantly above average. Assuming that her self-reporting is fairly accurate, we can say she needs to do something to improve her stress level. But what?

Kim's Relational Stress number—30—jumps out. That's way above average and well above the other two areas. The Personal Stress number is just above the average level, too.

Kim's Stress Events score is about average. She can't blame her high stress level on a one-time occurrence, so we know she won't heal naturally from this stress. She has to do something to change her life.

Finally, her Aggravators are quite high and her Fitness a bit low. It may not seem like much, but mathematically she's increasing her stress pile by more than a third of its original size. If she could even get these two numbers to a 1:1 ratio, she'd have a final score of 91, which is a nice improvement. She could probably cope with her Relational Stress pretty well if she reduced her Aggravators and increased her Fitness.

What's her agenda, then?

1. Work to improve her Relational Stress.
2. Improve stress Fitness.
3. Get rid of some Aggravators.

Back to the Questions

Once you've developed your broad agenda, go back through the test question by question. Take note of any place where your response was at the high-stress end—4s or 5s on environment and aggravator questions, or 1s or 2s on fitness questions—and circle the number of the question. Do this even if the whole area is not a problem for you. For example, you may have all 1s on the aggravators—except you're a terrible procrastinator, so question 31 got a 5. Your total score for aggravators is still pretty good, but that one answer jumps out, so circle question 31.

Once you've done this, you'll want to check out our specific suggestions as we go through the test, question by question, throughout the rest of this book. You may want to read every page of this book, but we don't mind if you skip to the discussions of your circled questions. Those are the pages that will help you the most.

Remember Kim? Her answers in her trouble area of relational stress indicate that she's in a bad marriage. Six of those eight questions got 4s or 5s from her, so she'll be thoroughly reading Part Three on Relational Stress. While her work environment and personal/community issues earned pretty low scores, she spiked up on questions 2 (change in the workplace) and 20 (concern for the future).

The two aggravators that hurt her most are questions 30 (being her own worst enemy) and 32 (taking on too much responsibility).

In the fitness area, Kim scored 1 on questions 35 (exercise), 36 (eating), and 44 (network of friends).

By focusing on these specific areas, she'll be able to fine-tune her agenda and develop an individual stress-management program. As you isolate your areas of stress, you'll be able to do the same.

Our suggestions cover a lot of topics—work habits, failing relationships, and personal attitudes, to name a few. Don't expect us to solve all those problems for you. This is a book about stress, and our suggestions are limited to reducing the stress associated with that situation. For instance, a troubled relationship can cause a lot of stress, as it does for Kim. This book won't give you much help in patching up that relationship. There are many other books (including some by us) that can help you in that area. This one focuses on relieving the stress of the situation.

Getting More Help

If you have serious stress problems, you may need more help than this book can give you. Look for these warning signs of dangerous stress:

- *Persistent problems eating or sleeping.* Not just one bad day or night, but if you've been having trouble for two weeks, see a doctor.
- *Physical problems.* Headaches, stomachaches, numbness, chronic fatigue, even nervous jitters—any of these could be a symptom of excessive stress. If these ills persist, get some help.
- *Emotional instability.* If you can't stop crying, or you're angrily yelling at everyone, stress may be the culprit. You need to see a counselor.

How do you find help for these ailments? Start with your physician. He or she can deal with your physical problems and may recommend a suitable stress counselor. Otherwise, ask your minister or friends or family members to recommend a good counselor. You might also want to check with your insurance provider to see if there's a list of approved counselors. If you still don't know where to turn, contact our Life Counseling office (1-800-882-2799 or www.lifecounseling.org). We may be able to direct you to a good counselor in your area.

PART TWO
Work Stress

MOST people spend about a third of their waking hours at work, counting weekends and everything. You get 168 hours each week and you're probably snoozing for about fifty. So if you're toiling away for a classic forty-hour workweek, that's a third of your life right there—not to mention the time you spend commuting to and from work, getting ready for work, thinking about work, or inventing excuses *not* to work.

Of course, some people put in considerably more hours. They're the first ones into the office, the last ones out. They take work home with them or travel the world on business. Or they work two or more jobs to make ends meet. Their workweeks total sixty, seventy, eighty hours. At a certain point, you stop working to live and you start living to work.

And let's not get too finicky on definitions here. "Work" is not necessarily a nine-to-five gig at an office or factory. You don't even have to get paid for it. Homemakers, students, and starving artists all work hard for little or no dough. And increasingly, people are working out of their homes, finding all sorts of novel ways to make a living. When you're working at home, the boundary lines blur. Living is working and working is living. It's hard to count up the hours.

But whatever your "work" is—office, factory, store, school, home, or on the road—it's probably stressful, at least to some degree.

1. On a scale from one to five, how would you rate the amount of stress you experience in the workplace?

THIS IS A CANOPY QUESTION. YOUR SCORE *should* INDICATE THE average of the other answers in this section, but it might not. The test asks about several common stressors in the workplace. You may be fine with all those factors, but you may have some different problem that makes your job severely stressful. Or maybe you face a lot of those common stressors, but you handle stress pretty well, so your overall sense of stress in the workplace is pretty low. Sometimes people get so accustomed to a certain stress level that they don't realize how stressed they are. They're gnawing through all their pencils, but they're saying, "No I'm not stressed, no way, not at all, not me." When you break down the stress to its individual factors (in questions 2 to 8), you may find you're more stressed than you think.

But remember that work is *supposed* to be stressful. Even if you love what you do, it's still work. It is the nature of work to impose stress on you. You have to accomplish certain things by a certain time in order to please certain people. Get that report to the boss by 3:30 or to the professor by Tuesday. Pick up the rec room in time to pick up the kids at school. Write the checks before payday or write that novel by Christmas. There's always something to do. And often there are time pressures, performance standards, self-doubt, and job insecurity to deal with. So it's no surprise that people tend to report more stress at work than in other environments.

That's not always bad. Many people seem to thrive on the high stress of their jobs. They live life at a certain pace and need pressure to stay in rhythm. If their desks aren't piled high with assignments, they get bored. When they give in and take vacations, it takes them a week and a half to slow down and start enjoying themselves.

Others, of course, can't handle that pressure. They stay in slower-paced, lower-pressure jobs. Or they drop out and start working for themselves, so the pace of their job can rise and fall according to their own biorhythms.

In our team of authors, Tom is the one who thrives on pressure. He runs a counseling office, meets with clients, speaks at seminars, teaches at a local college, edits newsletters, and hosts a radio show—when he's not writing books. Give him any down time and he's thinking up new projects. He just likes to have a lot to do.

"Just one of your days would choke me," one of Tom's colleagues recently told him. She's a homemaker, caring for two small children, and she works part-time at the counseling center. Obviously, her job isn't any easier; it just has a different pace, and a different kind of pressure.

Coauthor Randy Petersen is a medium-stress guy. Years ago, he had a full-time job editing three professional newsletters— four big deadlines every month. Now he's a free-lance writer, working at home, setting his own schedule. Oh, he gears up for deadlines, but he can't maintain a frenetic pace for long. He responds best to an ebb and flow of stress in his work life.

But we once worked with a man who had an extremely low tolerance for stress. If he had a lunch appointment, he'd mark out most of the afternoon. When things got tense around the office, he'd take the rest of the day off. He always looked calm, but that was because he avoided stress like the plague.

Water seeks its own level, and so do people. They tend to flow toward their optimum level of job stress. Fast-paced workers don't stay in slow-paced jobs. They keep looking until they find a stress level that fits them. Like Tom, they invent new things to do, adding new pressures when work gets slow. On the other hand, easygoing workers quit or get fired from fast-paced jobs. They can't stand the heat, so they stay out of the kitchen—or get thrown out. They find more comfortable employment elsewhere. Over time, people gravitate to appropriate stress levels.

Difficulties occur during times of transition. You take a new job, which turns out to have all sorts of pressures you hadn't expected. Your business grows, which is great, except now you have twice as much work to do in half as much time. Your company downsizes around you, and you have to take on the responsibilities of three people. You get a new boss, who tries to impose a whole different working rhythm on you. Or you grow older and can't quite handle the pace of your younger days.

Changes like these create new stress you didn't bargain for. The stress level you were used to has heightened. Suddenly, you feel new pressure day after day after day. And there doesn't seem to be any escape. You could quit your job, but that would unleash a host of *more* stressful situations. You're stuck.

What to do?

Throughout the rest of the book, we'll make suggestions for each of the questions on the Stress Test. The ideas for this "canopy" question will be pretty broad, but look for specifics in the other problem areas of the work section.

Clear out the stress in other areas of your life. If you have a high-stress job and there's no easy way to make it less stressful, then make sure your personal life has much less stress. Keep an even keel in your relationships, in your community life, in your own attitude. The great thing about learning your Stress Quotient is that you have several ways to ease your stress. You can cut yourself some slack for a high-stress job by going low stress in your other environments, by attacking your aggravators, or by improving your fitness.

Mentally take control. Dr. James E. Loehr has made a career of studying stress and success, among athletes as well as business people. He asserts that the problem is not in our stress, but in ourselves—in our emotional response to stress. "Stress does not damage us if we are in control," he says, citing a Yale experiment on lab rats.[1] Two rats were given electric shocks at random intervals, but one of the rats had a lever that could turn off the current. Though both rats received the same amount of shock, the controlling rat stayed healthy. The other rat went batty.

When you feel like a lab rat at work, your problem is not the daily shocks to your system, but the idea that you have no control. Others are making the decisions and forcing you to jump through hoops. But how would things change if you convinced yourself that you were ultimately in control? Of course you'll have bosses telling you what to do, but you could always quit. You don't quit because you need the job, your family needs the money, and your house has two mortgages—but that just means that you're deciding to stay employed. It's up to you. Each day, you're making the choice to work there. Ultimately, you are in control.

Renegotiate your situation. Perhaps you can change the things about your job that are giving you the most stress. Talk to your boss or coworkers to see if you can make less stressful arrangements. Let them know how stress is affecting your life and your work. If you're close to quitting, say so.

The fact is, often little things create the stress that drives us bonkers. The boss's last-second changes. The meetings where you really don't need to be. The volume of the phone's ring. The way the vice-president keeps calling you "Tiger." A little communication might just clear up these problems.

Or not. But at least you've taken control of your situation and made an effort to improve things.

Ease a transition. Then again, you could quit. If your current work environment is dangerously stressful, you may have no other option. But as we mentioned earlier, quitting a stressful job can make your life still more stressful—unless you prepare for it. If you decide you need to quit, start looking for your next job six months to a year in advance. Can you stay in the stressful job another year? Probably. And now that you've decided to leave, you'll feel more in control. That extra time will help you zero in on the best opportunity, without the panic of a sudden job loss. As you do your job search, pay special attention to the stress level of your new position. Use vacation time or personal days to do interviews. And save up your money. Gear up your family for any changes they'll need to make. Make the whole transition as easy as possible—for everyone.

2. How much change do you experience in the workplace, such as instability, fluctuating job requirements, or an erratic boss?

A GENERATION AGO, PEOPLE OFTEN WORKED FOR THE SAME COM-
pany for fifty years and got a gold watch when they retired. During
that time they'd rise in the ranks, but changes were generally slow.
Many workers at age sixty were doing pretty much the same things
they were doing at age thirty.

Times have changed. Now people flit from company to company on their way up the corporate ladder. Businesses often
downsize to stay competitive, tightening their payrolls and in the
process abandoning loyal employees. And the jobs themselves are
changing. If you learned any sort of technical skill as late as the
70s, it's already obsolete, as computers have totally retooled the
workplace. If you haven't kept up, you've been left behind.

Computers and other technological advances have increased
the speed of everything we do. In our microwave age, it seems
to take forever when you have to roast something in a conventional oven. Speed dialing allows us to punch one button instead
of eleven (or more!) to connect with our loved ones. And people
upgrade their modems because they're tired of waiting twenty
seconds to download a file they could get in ten.

In the workplace it's even more noticeable. Time is money,
and the deadlines are fast and furious. First came the delivery
revolution. FedEx and its ilk could put our info on others' desks
the next morning. Now e-mail can do it instantly. You used to
be able to relax a bit after the FedEx office closed; now you can
work all night if you need to. That's progress?! Teleconferencing
lets you meet daily with cross-country clients you used to visit
once a year. And the Internet puts tons of information at your
fingertips—much more than you need, and certainly more than
you have the time to sort through.

Commerce careens at ever-growing speeds. And that means
that changes are happening suddenly in your workplace, without much warning.

"Forget traditional distribution," the boss says. "We're going on the Internet." And with that word, your whole department has to learn a whole new task. Everything you've been working on for the last five years can now be shredded. It's a new ballgame. Can you handle it?

The burgeoning of new markets and new media sometimes means that people are forced into positions where they don't know what they're doing. It seems that *everybody* is struggling uphill on the learning curve. There are about 300 Internet experts in the world. A hundred work for Microsoft, another hundred for AOL, and the other hundred are thirteen-year-olds. Seriously though, with technology zooming ahead of training, you may be put in charge of an area where you have no clue. Learn quickly. The company doesn't have time for mistakes.

Worse yet, your boss may be put in charge of a new area, and he or she may have no clue about what to do. Maybe your boss is brilliant and always coming up with new ideas which are significantly different from yesterday's ideas—and of course it's up to you to implement them. Or maybe your boss is neurotic, always second-guessing. It can be extremely stressful trying to keep up with an energetic boss or trying to clean up after a disorganized one. You need to be a mind reader and a miracle worker.

Change is always stressful, whether you're dealing with a changing business, a changing job description, or the changing mind of your boss. We are creatures of habit; it's always tough to adjust.

What to do?

If changes in your workplace are overstressing you, what options do you have? You're certainly not going to hold back the march of progress. Your business will computerize, digitize, laserize, and hop on the information superhighway. Changes will happen. You can't do anything about that, but you can change yourself and your attitude.

Make friends with change. You may be one of those people who resist any change at all. If so, then you've got a major mind-control project ahead of you. Loosen up! Learn to love change in the rest of your life, and then maybe your changing workplace won't be so stressful. Wear something weird to work. Take a different train. Play chess with your kids, only let them make up the rules as they go along (they will anyway).

Spend extra time on the learning curve. Devote some extra hours to studying new things you need to know at work. Take a night course. Or get out the manual and master that computer program. An extra hour spent now can make all your working hours more comfortable. What's more, learning can be fun—but not when you're under the gun. That's why you need to find extra time, non-work time, to get yourself up to speed.

Know your limits. Don't take on a new responsibility just because "someone has to." You have a finite amount of time and energy. If you add a new task, you have to subtract something else. (Try to talk your boss into this same philosophy.)

Communicate clearly. One problem with rapid change is that misunderstandings arise easily. New challenges require new approaches, which may or may not be like the old approaches. Your boss and coworkers may assume different things, and that may put you in a bind—unless you're always talking it out. Part of clear communication may be getting it in writing. Jot down your boss's instructions, especially if those instructions may change within a few hours.

Reset every day. One problem with rapid change in the workplace: You fear you'll lose everything you've gained. And maybe you will. Say a new company takes over yours, bringing in their own staff. If you manage to keep a job, you're bumped a few rungs down. All your ladder climbing of the last five years is erased. But that doesn't mean your life has been erased. Every day you gain experience, knowledge, goodwill. These are things no one can take from you. If you start every day by welcoming the chance to take the next step and not resting on past laurels, the turbulence of the marketplace won't devastate you.

3. How vulnerable do you feel in the workplace, such as fearing a layoff, feeling unsafe, or in some other way threatened?

HARRY GOT FIRED FOR CHALLENGING HIS BOSS'S UNETHICAL CON-
duct. As the chief financial officer for the company, he thought
he might talk some sense into the CEO. Instead he got canned.

It was the right thing to do, but Harry kept wondering if it
might have been better to keep quiet. Now his whole life was in
upheaval. How would he pay the mortgage on his fine, suburban
home? How would he pay college tuition for his two daughters?

He sent out his résumé, but at his level, jobs were hard to
come by. He dug into his savings and bought a business he knew
nothing about. That was a mistake—he lost a bundle. Finally
he landed a job that paid less than his previous position. Still, it
was a job. He just wasn't sure how long it would last.

Three years ago, at his old job, Harry felt secure. He took
the train every day, crunched his numbers, came back home, and
sank into the recliner. Life was good. But then everything fell apart.
This new job may be wonderful, but Harry isn't sure.

This episode has had too many reruns in modern life. With
the business world hurtling forward at light speed, job security
is becoming extinct. No matter how well you do your job, no
matter how valuable you are to the company, no matter what the
bottom line, you could lose your job tomorrow. If your job is ten-
uous, you need to know that and deal with it. Job loss isn't
something to worry about—just something to prepare for.

Other people may feel vulnerable at their jobs for different reasons. Maybe you're working the graveyard shift at a gas station.
We knew one woman who landed a job at a city hospital—which
was great, except she had to walk three blocks to and from the
parking lot, through a tough neighborhood.

And some people just have dangerous jobs. Working with
big machinery or with toxic substances, you're never far from the
possibility of death or injury. Despite official safety standards,
employees may feel threatened by the natural risk involved in
their daily work.

Sexual harassment can also be a threat. Some women (and, more rarely, men) may fear being pressured or even attacked by a boss or coworker. Even if the danger isn't physical, you could suffer demotion, severe embarrassment, or damage to your reputation. Many companies have enacted protective policies, and there are new laws on the subject, but sexual harassment is still a big mess, and victims suffer greatly. Our friend Christine saw a good work environment shattered when a male coworker made a pass at her and grabbed her breast. Her complaint launched a "he said/she said" debate that ended in the loss of her job.

What to do?

All sorts of threats can disrupt the calm of your working environment, adding stress to your daily life. If you scored high on this question, take stock of your fears and see what you can do to alleviate them.

Evaluate the threat. What, specifically, are you afraid of? Do you fear the loss of your job? Or is it an issue of physical safety? Many fears can grow as long as they're vague, but when you actually name them, they take on reasonable proportions. Once you've named the fear, try to ascertain its seriousness. Talk with your boss or coworkers about the situation. Do they have similar fears? Do they think you're being paranoid or just careful?

Improve your position. If you're afraid of losing your job, start looking for a new one. Or make yourself so indispensable that your company has to keep you. We know psychologists who worry about the effects of managed care on the counseling profession — so they're taking computer courses on the side, just in case they need to launch a new career.

If you're concerned about physical safety, take steps to safeguard yourself. Don't work alone late at night. Walk in groups, adopt extra safety precautions, develop a safety checklist. Don't trust your company to protect you; take responsibility for your own well-being.

If you're worried about sexual harassment or some other interpersonal dispute, improve your position by establishing friendships among your coworkers. Win their trust by proving yourself trust-worthy. Find your allies in the workplace. If you have concerns about the behavior of particular coworkers toward you, share these concerns with your allies. Don't go it alone.

Take it upstairs. Don't be afraid to discuss your fears with your superiors. If there are safety issues at work, your boss needs to know about them. Perhaps additional safety measures can be instituted. But even if you're worried about job security, your boss might be able to give you the assurances you need — or sugges-tions about how to improve your position or prepare for the future.

Turn your fears to cheers. All right, it's hard to do this with issues of physical safety or harassment, but if job security is a problem, look on the bright side. Even if you lose your job, that might open up a whole new opportunity for you. Don't cling so tightly to your present position that you can't grasp the gifts of the future.

4. Do you sense a lack of control on your job, such as an inability to effect change or inability to have an impact on the decisions that are made?

CATHY WORKS IN A COFFEE SHOP. SHE LOVES IT, BUT SHE ALSO FINDS it very frustrating. It's clear that she could run the place. She trains many of the new employees, and she treats each customer with a proprietary energy. Every moment she's there, she's sweeping the floor or scraping the grill, brewing a fresh pot, or pouring another cup for a customer—just as if she ran the place. But she doesn't.

Zelda, the manager, has different ideas about the shop. Though money is tight, Zelda wants to spend it on decorations. "People won't come if the place doesn't look nice," she says. But Cathy thinks those expenditures are frivolous. "Why can't we spend that money to serve better food?" she wonders.

Cathy figured out the most efficient way to arrange the serving area, and she dutifully puts everything in its place—spoons, cups, coffee, and so on. Then Zelda rearranged things. Cathy is convinced that Zelda did this just to bug her. So, at the beginning of her shift, she changes everything from Zelda's way to her own way. When Zelda comes in, she undoes everything Cathy set up. And so it goes.

What's the problem here? Cathy cares too much. She has thrown her life into this shop, and she desperately wants it to succeed—but she's not the owner or manager. Ultimately, she has no control over how money is spent, what food is served, or how the place is advertised. She can make suggestions, but (given her track record with Zelda) those suggestions are often ignored. As a result, Cathy feels considerable stress at her job.

In his book, *Stress for Success*, stress doctor James E. Loehr notes, "The perception of an event being beyond one's control is associated with distress, depression, and a variety of other health risks."[2] The control factor, he says, is what turns good stress to bad stress. Stress can be very good for us, especially in competitive situations. It becomes a problem (*dis*-stress) when we feel that we can't control what's happening. "The only way to survive and thrive in your world," Loehr adds, "is not to get rid of stress, but to be in control."

Unless you're the boss, however, you're not in control of your workplace. But if you don't have the final say, it helps to have *some* say. Work is less stressful when you have some input into the decisions that affect you. That's the genius behind the age-old suggestion box. Companies have committee meetings, profit-sharing plans, employee ownership, and even unions as ways of sharing the control and keeping workers happy. Even if your ideas aren't always accepted, you work better knowing that your opinion matters. It becomes *your* business, not just the company you work for.

Many writers documented the incredible stress felt by workers and citizens in Communist regimes, where distant bureaucrats made decisions and there were severe consequences for nonconformity. Even there, people managed to keep their dignity by finding some small area of life in which they could make their own decisions. Presumably democracy is much less stressful. Our government officials may madden us, but we can always throw the rascals out next November.

"Live free or die" was a slogan of American revolutionaries in the 1770s. It fits equally well in the twenty-first century. When all our decisions are made for us, when we have no control, we feel a deadening stress — or we fight with a revolutionary fervor, grabbing control that no one has given us.

What to do?

If feeling out of control causes you stress, you need to start feeling in control. You don't actually need to possess any more control, you just need to feel that way. So this may involve some mind games, some self-talk, some revision of your vision.

Play politics. Every organization has its own ways of getting things done. If it's important for you to gain some input in the decisions of your company, find out which people have the power and figure out how to influence them. We don't mean to be too Machiavellian here, but it's important to learn the channels of power where you work. This may be as simple as a chat with your boss's secretary or treating the mailroom personnel as real human beings. The real flow of power may be quite different from the organizational hierarchy. Study it for a while to find who the opinion leaders are. What kind of official and unofficial "suggestion boxes" does your business have? How can you get your ideas to the people who need to hear them?

Find your province. You may never have a lot of influence in the major decisions of your company, but you might find a small area that you can control. Maybe you can run your department or edit your newsletter or just organize your desk. Whatever it is, try to find at least one area where your decisions really matter.

The personal computer specialists at IBM in the 1970s had to be terribly frustrated. The company was heavily invested in mainframes—that was the future of computing, as far as they were concerned. But they allowed their PC department to function independently, and the rest is history. IBM's PC people found their province and they took control of it as best they could. As a result, they dragged the rest of their company into the future as the IBM PC became the standard for popular computing.

Control yourself. Even if you have no control over anyone or anything else, you can always control yourself. No one else can tell you how to think or feel, even if they give you dumb work to do. So be creative about your own approach to your work. Find challenges. Take pride in how efficiently, how cheerfully, how creatively you complete the most mundane tasks. Learn to expect a constantly changing flow of assignments, completely out of your control, but then work at "going with the flow" and dealing with those erratic expectations. You can't control the input, but you can control your response to it.

Establish rituals. If you're finding it hard to gain a sense of control at work, try some new rituals. Get to work at a certain time each day, perhaps ten or fifteen minutes early. Use those extra moments to create a to-do list, to prepare the supplies you'll need, or to pray. Take a mid-morning or mid-afternoon exercise break, walking up and down the stairs or around the block. Take control of what you eat and drink before, during, and after work. See if you can set aside certain times of each day for certain tasks.

Rituals give your mind and body a sense of order, easing your stress. They also give you a greater sense of control.

Be a team player. You may want more control than you should have. If you're always convinced that you have *the* idea that's going to turn your company around, if you're always saying that everyone else is an idiot, if you are always suggesting solutions for everyone else's problems—well, no wonder no one's listening to you! You deserve some input, but others do too. Be humble about your own contributions and be willing to listen to your coworkers. At most workplaces, the best ideas are culled from many different suggestions and developed in a team process. Allow yourself to be part of a team.

5. Do you have a heavy workload and find that you can't complete tasks on schedule?

WHEN ANITA WAS OFFERED A NEW JOB, SHE JUMPED AT IT. AS AN editor for a religious publication, she had enjoyed a low-key environment, but not the low pay that went with it. Then she met a well-respected CEO who needed a media manager. She had to move across the country, but her salary more than doubled. Her responsibilities also broadened. Instead of just packaging a bimonthly magazine, Anita was writing scripts for a daily radio program, articles for a biweekly magazine column and a monthly newsletter, as well as occasional speeches. Every day her plate was full. And if her work wasn't up to snuff, the CEO insisted on a rewrite. He was a good, kind man, but he demanded excellence in every part of his organization. If that meant she had to work late, come to the office on weekends, or take work home with her, so be it. That's what they were paying her for.

Stress was just part of the job.

Thousands of workers could tell similar stories about how they climbed the corporate ladder to the corporate stratosphere — the "stressosphere," you might call it. Suddenly, they can afford a beautiful home, an expensive car or two, a luxurious vacation — but they can't afford the time to enjoy all their possessions. They don't dare complain about the stress, because a dozen junior executives are yapping at their heels. When it comes to job stress, you get what you get paid for.

Some jobs are very demanding, and some fields are especially stressful. If you work on a daily newspaper, you have a deadline every day. If you work on Wall Street, you'd better be ready when the bell rings. If you work for the post office, you have to make your appointed rounds.

And there are certain companies in all types of business that foster a high-stress environment. Maybe the boss just likes it that way, as in Anita's new job. Maybe people are convinced that pressure creates productivity. Maybe you just have a Type-A personality on top, and that attitude trickles down through the whole company.

But it could be you, not the company. Certain people give

themselves too much work to do, habitually biting off more than they can chew. You get bored if your to-do list isn't a page-and-a-half long. Or you think up more projects than you can get to. Maybe you have that old Protestant work ethic deeply rooted in you, and you keep trying to validate your existence by getting stuff done. But then your perfectionism makes you go back and redo the stuff you already did, so you never really finish anything.

Or maybe you just like to work hard.

Leslie runs a small company with about fifteen employees. "We can't grow any larger," she says, "because I just can't handle any more work." Every one of those fifteen employees reports to Leslie. She can't take a day off, because her workers rely on her for their marching orders. Why doesn't she train people to take leadership responsibility? "No, I'm the only one who can run this company," she says. "I couldn't trust anyone else to do what I do."

This story is played out in many businesses that revolve around one person. The boss may have built a thriving company on personal charisma and market smarts, but if he or she can't delegate leadership responsibility, the company's growth gets stalled. The boss's desk is only so big. The leader may be working twenty hours a day, and demanding similar commitment from everyone else, and still there's frustration because the company can't grow. The company is held back because the boss won't let go of the reins.

But having too much to do isn't just a problem for executives. At all levels, there are employees who take too much responsibility, who take on tasks that are literally none of their business. A secretary we know went into a panic when a toilet overflowed in a company rest room. She didn't know how to fix it, but she felt she had to try. Instead of just calling maintenance and letting the experts take care of it, she wasted an hour of her secretarial time and needlessly increased her stress level.

Sure, it's nice when someone cares enough about the company to go the extra mile. You don't want a workplace filled with people who throw up their hands and say, "That's not my job." But when your work is getting hectic, that's exactly what you need to say. If you're having a hard time keeping up with things that are in your job description, why take on extra responsibilities that aren't?

What to do?

Your response to an overwhelming workload depends on whether these tasks are given to you or whether you choose them yourself. That is, how much control do you have over your assignments? But then there's also the matter of demand and production. You can reduce your workload by getting rid of some tasks, or getting them done. Perhaps you can get ahead by working more efficiently.

Communicate. If you're getting an unreasonable pile of projects dumped on your desk, you need to talk with your boss about it. Don't expect a lot of sympathy. Your boss may say, "If you can't do the job, I'll find someone who can." But a smart supervisor will recognize the value of your feedback. If you are genuinely working as hard as you can and you're still overwhelmed, the boss simply needs to give you less to do. Or perhaps the boss will suggest better ways to accomplish your tasks. Maybe, seeing the big picture, your supervisor will redistribute the assignments so that your whole department works together more efficiently. Sometimes the people handing out the work have no idea how much time it takes to do the work. You can help the whole process by communicating your progress honestly.

Plan ahead. Do all you can to foresee a heavy workload and prepare for it. If you know a big project starts Monday, get plenty of rest that weekend. Farm out some of your chores, cancel some social engagements, tell friends not to call you for a while. Make sure you're not overwhelmed by extraneous matters.

Prioritize. What must be done? What should be done? What could be done, but only if you have time? What task could wait for tomorrow, or next week, or next month? Follow that great adage: "Never do today what you can put off till tomorrow." Seriously, if your workload is a sinking ship and you're rowing like mad, you might have to throw some tasks overboard. If you can shirk a task for a period of time, then do it. Put it on your calendar for next April and don't think about it until then. Ask your supervisor for help in prioritizing your tasks. He or she may then see the enormity of your workload as well as your desire to accomplish things. And obviously you'll be on the same page about the relative importance of these tasks.

Delegate. If you have some control over your workload, you have several remedies. The first is to delegate responsibilities to others. Leslie, the boss who can't take a day off, needs to learn this. Hand off to others the jobs you can't do yourself. You may want to retain an overseeing responsibility, but be careful not to get drawn into *doing* the things you've delegated. Remember, there will be a learning curve, a period of time when your "delegate" won't do the job as well or as quickly as you could. But you'll get past that, and everyone's productivity will increase. And that will ease your workload.

Estimate wisely. We know one office worker who routinely underestimates the time it takes to do things. He's smart and fast and generally good at what he does, but he expects too much of himself. A task others might do in an hour, he can do in 45 minutes, but he'll promise it in 30 minutes. So he's always pushing himself, taking on twice as many assignments as others, and always apologizing for breaking his promises. If you're in a position to plan your workload, make sure you make reasonable estimates of the time each task will take. And don't take the best-case scenario. Build in break time, thinking time, and time for unexpected things to go wrong.

Observe boundaries. Look at your workload and see which tasks might easily fall into the jurisdiction of others around you. Have you taken on responsibilities that don't really belong to you? That was the problem of the secretary who tried to fix the toilet. She should have said, "That's not my job." When appropriate, you should say the same.

Know where your talents lie. There are some things you can do very well, other things you can't. Look at your pile of stuff to do and find the things you don't do well. Wherever possible, hand these jobs off to those who excel in those things. You might even trade some tasks you don't do well for some you're great at. Jim, for example, hates calling people on the phone. When he has to make phone calls, he gets tense, he worries that he's interrupting some important business on the other end of the line, he hopes that he'll get a machine (and not have to bother some real person). Irrational, maybe, but Jim is a lousy phone caller. So when Jim is organizing projects for work or for his extracurricular projects, he always tries to find people who like to use the phone. He gladly writes up extra reports if someone else will make the calls.

Learn to say no. You want to be a nice guy. People come to you with an urgent need and ask you to meet it. How can you turn them down? Well, if you're already up to your temples in work—to the point that you're overstressed and your health is threatened—you have to say no. Practice it. Put your tongue on the roof of your mouth and make a sound—NNNNN—that's good. Now round your mouth in a vowel sound—OOOOOO. N-O. No! You can do it. Try it again. We know one big-hearted executive who made it a rule never to agree to do anything on the same day he was asked. That removed him from the emotional pressure of staring into the puppy-dog eyes of a friend asking a favor. He would just respond, "Sorry, I never say yes on the same day. Let me sleep on it. I'll let you know tomorrow." Then he could make a rational decision whether he could add this favor to his to-do list.

Find an extra work block. As we said, you can also ease the stress of an overwhelming workload by getting more of it done. One option: find a four-hour block of time to tackle things you couldn't do in your normal work time. If you can do this, you must plan it well. Maybe working late one night in the office, without meetings, phone calls, or interruptions, will be extremely productive. Maybe you could take work home and shut yourself off from distractions (good luck!). Maybe you could borrow someone else's office for a weekend or evening block of time. You might even consider renting a hotel room to get away from distractions. It may sound strange to combat work stress by doing more work, but if you can gut it out for one distinct block of time and get ahead in your work, you can substantially ease your job pressures. But if this becomes a weekly occurrence, and you're working every Saturday and Sunday, it defeats the purpose.

Take breaks. We aren't meant to work nonstop. Human beings need to eat, sleep, take walks around the block, and chat with friends. You can come back to your work refreshed from each of these activities, and your greater productivity will make up for the work time you lost. Know your own rhythms and follow them. Take a mid-morning coffee break with your coworkers, but don't talk about work. Take a walk at lunchtime (and watch out for lunch meetings that are more work than relaxation). Figure out the warning signs of job fatigue and learn what to do to refresh yourself. Don't pamper yourself too much, though. We knew one self-employed copywriter who would work for an hour and then "rest up" with a two-hour trip to the mall—not very productive. *Short* breaks can be very effective at helping you to work better.

Watch aggravators. A later chapter will deal in depth with stress aggravators—those stress-induced habits that make things worse. Some people try to escape from a heavy workload by, say, getting drunk after work. That might ease your pain for a few hours, but it will steal valuable recovery time from you and probably keep you from being fully productive the next day. Your aggravator may be different, but they all have one thing in common: They promise to ease your stress, but they just make it worse.

6. How poor is the communication in your workplace, such as vague goals and objectives, or unclear expectations?

COMMUNICATION IS A HUGE PROBLEM IN LARGE COMPANIES. AS MUCH as the CEOs trumpet "mission statements" or "core values," workers in the trenches often don't know what's going on. What are we really trying to accomplish here? If that question is not answered, workers can feel that their work is meaningless—and that adds stress.

In an ancient myth, a man named Sisyphus was condemned to roll a giant boulder up a steep hill. Once he reached the top, the boulder rolled down the other side, so he had to start all over. Sadly, that matches the job description for many workers today. They have no sense of accomplishment, because no one has communicated what their work is about.

Large companies are especially plagued with communication problems because there are so many links in the chain. If one vice-president, middle manager, or foreman communicates poorly, then a whole department may stay in the dark. But smaller companies may suffer too, if a boss fails to present the big picture and establish clear objectives for the employees.

Without proper communication, workers can waste effort by duplicating the work of others. Worse yet, one department might be working hard to undo what another department is doing. Nothing is more disheartening than to work hard on a project that is ultimately scuttled because of poor communication.

Some employees get frustrated because they don't know how creative they're allowed to be. "Create a brochure," the boss barks to the publicity person. *How? What kind?* she wonders, but the boss expects her to read his mind. So she works hard to write and design a stunning brochure. When she plunks it on the boss's desk, however, he says, "It's all wrong. This isn't what I wanted at all." So the next time she gets a project, she doesn't know how much effort to put into it. *Maybe this will be all wrong too,* she worries. She feels the stress of uncertainty, always afraid that she's not doing her job well enough, because no one has told her what she needs to do.

Savvy employees learn when to ask for direction, but often bosses don't want to be bothered. One personnel manager told us of the stress he felt over an employee newsletter he prepared. The boss insisted on okaying it before it went out, but the newsletter would get lost on the boss's desk for weeks. Deadlines would pass. Polite reminders to the boss went unanswered. Finally, in desperation, he reprinted some old material the boss had okayed years earlier. When he heard (secondhand, of course) that the boss was unhappy with the quality of that newsletter, the personnel manager hit the roof. He prepared a detailed report of his attempts to communicate and the boss's total lack of response. That, too, probably got lost on the boss's desk. A month later, with no hope of better communication, the manager quit.

Businesses often have bottlenecks, where approval is needed but slow to appear. Certain desks become "black holes," where memos are lost at the bottom of an ever-growing pile. E-mail may speed up communication in some corners of commerce, but a computer message can be ignored as easily as a written note—and it can be quickly erased.

Poor communication can cause stress in many areas of life, but business is one of the worst. It comes back to the issue of control. Without proper communication, you have no way of knowing whether you're doing what you must do to succeed. You feel you have no control over your future. And that's stressful.

What to do?

Proper communication is a two-way street, of course. You may be communicating as thoroughly as possible *to* someone but not receiving any communication *from* that person. That's frustrating. Still, you can do a few things that might open the lines. And if that doesn't work, there are some ways to ease the stress of noncommunication.

Catch the vision. If you're toiling without purpose in the bowels of a bureaucracy, try to enlarge your vision. Think about what your company (or your department) is doing and why. Consider your own role in all of that. If you get a clear picture of your organization's overall goals, you should find it easier making decisions to help meet those goals.

Practice mind reading. If your boss expects you to be a mind reader, be one! Analyze the kind of work he or she has praised or panned and figure out what your boss likes. You may still need to ask for approval on certain projects, but you're more apt to get it if you learn to think like the higher-ups.

Ask for a report card. When Ed Koch was mayor of New York City, he'd go around the city asking people, "How am I doing?" He figured that the citizens were ultimately his employers, so he needed to get their feedback. Maybe you can do the same with your employer, especially if communication seems to be lacking. Most bosses appreciate an employee who asks, "How can I do a better job?"

Do your own thing. Pretend that you're your own boss. Think about the goals of the company and your own personal goals. Draw up a task list, present it to your boss, and say, "Here's what I want to accomplish in the next three months. Is this a good plan?" If you're not getting enough direction, direct yourself. This should ease the stressful paralysis of not knowing what to do. You'll be taking matters into your own hands—until you're instructed to do otherwise.

Provide a fail-safe. In cases of severe communication breakdown and after many conventional tries at getting feedback, you may need to present your requests in a negative way. "If I don't hear from you by Friday, I'll go ahead and . . . " If your boss doesn't like what you go ahead and do, well, tough—you offered an opportunity to correct it. Be sure you allow a reasonable time for response, and don't do anything you would expect to be disapproved. Make sure you keep a copy of your written attempts for approval. Of course, depending on the dynamics of your work situation, this may not protect you from the consequences if your boss has second thoughts.

Try different methods. Some people just don't like the telephone. They prefer meeting face to face. Others won't remember anything you say face to face, so you have to write it down. Some put written memos in piles that won't be excavated until the year 2525, so it's better to send e-mail. Others still haven't connected with e-mail. They let messages pile up and then they erase them, rather than sorting between junk mail and the messages you've been frantically sending. If communication is a problem with certain people in your workplace, figure out how they receive messages best. Try different times of day—many executives are fresh early in the day and sluggish after lunch. Others don't check messages until the end of the day—so don't freak out if you don't get an immediate response.

Learn the language. People talk—and hear—in different ways. Some are apologetic, others dogmatic. Some use I-language ("I think that's a good idea"); others use we-language ("We're all agreed then that this is a good idea"); still others use you-language ("If you don't use this idea, you're crazy"). Some people "think out loud" while others develop their thoughts in private and then share only their findings. Deborah Tannen has written widely on gender differences in communication, something else to consider if you're having trouble sending or receiving messages at work. After detailing a number of differences that are often gender-related (such as an apologetic tone, indirectness, asking for directions), Tannen sums up with a plea to pay more attention to conversational style: "Understanding what goes on when people talk to each other is the best way to improve communication—and get more work done—in the workplace as in all aspects of our lives."[3]

Learn to let go. At a certain point, it's just not worth worrying about. If you're not getting the communication you need and you've done everything you can to improve the situation, then just do your job and don't sweat it. It's not your problem. Find your fulfillment in hobbies or relationships—or look for another job. Our friend Bill works for a government agency that's notorious for its shoddy communication. "No one cares," he says. So he puts in his time and then comes home to work on an airplane he's building. That's right—just a little project he's doing on his own that gives him great satisfaction, putting together a real plane. He still hates his job, but he gets his personal sense of accomplishment from his hobby; and he's got his résumé out.

Of course you want to do good work, and your uncommunicative boss or coworkers may be hindering you, but you'll just hurt yourself more if you stew about it. For your own sanity, it's all right to stop caring about the end result of your labors. Pull your focus in. Be meticulous about your own work. And you may need to protect yourself by keeping records of your attempts to communicate. But let the rest go.

7. How responsible are you for the well-being and/or the job performance of others?

NOTICE THAT WE'RE NOT ASKING WHETHER THE PEOPLE WHO answer to you are good, loyal workers or rebellious slackers. That will make some difference in your stress level, but the very fact that you're in charge of somebody is a significant stressor, even if they're model employees.

Why? It comes back to the issue of control. You can't determine what your people will ultimately do, and yet you're responsible for them. They have free choice, to work hard or not, to be careful or not, to make mistakes or not—and you have to live with the consequences.

The best example of this comes not from the world of business, but from the home. Parents are responsible for the well-being of their children, and for their actions. As kids grow, they move farther and farther out of the protective reach of their parents. They can cross the street on their own. They can hang out with friends after school. They can go on a school trip. They can borrow the car. At each point, the parents have less control, but just as much responsibility.

One mother tells of the experience of helping her daughter ride a bicycle for the first time. She ran alongside with support and encouragement until the girl was pedaling and steering on her own, riding down the street and around the corner. Then . . . panic. The mother was sure her daughter had fallen, crashed into something, been hit by a car. The weight of responsibility was awesome, until the girl came riding back, beaming.

In this respect, the stay-at-home mom faces the same challenge as the CEO. Both depend on their charges to make good choices. You can offer instruction, cast a vision, give a pep talk, and support it all with disciplinary review—but eventually it's out of your hands. At all levels of the workplace, leaders have that experience. The coach sends the players on the field, the director puts actors on stage, the foreman places workers on the line, the lawyer assigns key research to an assistant. If you're a leader, you gulp, you pray, you cross your fingers, you shout instructions, and then you see what happens.

If you're a people pleaser, that just makes it worse. You're responsible for people, but you also want them to like you. You have to crack the whip sometimes, but you still want to be a nice guy. That's not easy. Parents like this find it hard to discipline their children. The thought that your kid might be hating you while sitting in the corner is horrendous. But if you're responsible to shape the child's behavior, sometimes you have to do the unpopular thing.

The same conflict applies in business. A leader may work at developing an easy camaraderie with employees, but that can make it harder to exert leadership. Sometimes rules must be enforced, standards must be adhered to, performance must be demanded—even if that makes you seem like a surly ogre.

A leader must also make decisions that favor one group or another, or one person over another. Which department gets the big contract? Which worker gets the promotion? Whatever your decision, someone's going to be mad at you. Do you accept this person's idea because you want the person to like you? No, you have to do what you think is best for the company, no matter how many toes you're stepping on. You're never going to please everyone.

This struggle reaches its peak when you have to let people go. Bill, the CEO of a small company, was delighted to hire his old buddy Mel as business manager. But after a few years it was obvious that Mel just wasn't working out, and the board began pressuring Bill to do something. It broke his heart, but Bill called Mel into his office and fired him. Sometimes responsibility hurts. When you're responsible for the whole, you can't be too connected to any individual part.

Leadership can take its toll on relationships, adding stress to a work situation. Karen was one of a tight-knit group of secretaries who was promoted to office manager. Her best friend Julie was happy for her, but over time their relationship changed. When Karen gave Julie a task that had to be done immediately, Julie would laugh at her. The implication was: "Hey, you're my best friend. I don't have to do what you say." Karen wasn't trying to put on airs, but she needed some respect, which she wasn't getting from Julie. Finally Julie resigned, largely because she found it so hard to work for her old chum. Even then, their friendship was irreparably damaged.

Many leaders have experienced this. Relationships change when leadership responsibility is added to the mix, no matter how humble the leader wants to be. Those changes create stress, and they can also rob a leader of an important method of stress relief. If you're used to going out after hours with some working buddies and complaining about the boss—well, that's a bit different when you *are* the boss.

What to do?

If you find yourself in a position of responsibility, you *will* have stress. You can't get rid of it entirely unless you give up that position. Still, you can manage the stress of the situation to keep it from overwhelming you.

Accept your role. If you have recently, like Karen, moved into a position of leadership, stop trying to be "one of the girls." The sooner you accept the change, the sooner the others will. That doesn't mean you have to become proud or domineering or surly. Let your same old personality shine through. Leadership doesn't make you any better than those who work for you, but in the context of your business it gives you certain power which you must wield for the good of the company.

Paraphrase Lincoln. Honest Abe supposedly said, "You may *fool* all the people some of the time . . . " We like to apply his dictum to people pleasing. Try this: "You may *please* all the people some of the time; you can even please some of the people all the time; but you can't please all of the people all the time." If you're stressed from trying to keep everyone happy, memorize this and recite it to yourself frequently.

Be up front about the situation. A lot of leadership stress is caused by uncertainty, false assumptions, mixed signals. If people pleasing is a problem for you, you may need to sit down with your workers and have a heart-to-heart talk. Let them know that you like them, but you're also in charge. "We all have to do what's best for the company, not what's best for ourselves. So I may ask you to do something you don't like, or I may shoot down your idea, or I may criticize something you've done—not because I don't like you or I think I'm better than you or anything like that— it's just my job."

Find a confidant. You need someone who understands the struggles of leadership. Even if you enjoy the people who work for you, don't use them as sounding boards for your leadership frustrations. It's best to find someone at a similar level of responsibility, and get together occasionally to blow off steam. (Usually a spouse is not the best confidant for work matters, because that stirs in a whole new set of relational issues.)

Enjoy the risk of people building. You have a responsibility to your business, but you also have a responsibility to the people who work for you. This tension creates stress. Do you, for instance, send the rookie on a sales trip instead of the over-worked veteran? If you're looking for an immediate payoff, the veteran is more likely to seal the deal. But if you're planning for the future, you need to keep the old-timer rested and the young buck challenged. Maybe the rookie doesn't make the sale, but he learns something in the process. You can manage the stress better if you understand people building as a key element of your job. (If you're a teacher or a parent, you already know that people building *is* your job.) This, of course, involves risk. We need failure as well as success—that's how people grow. People building is risky business, but the great thing is that, even when you fail, you succeed. Sure, you need to plan the risks so that the rewards are maximized and the penalties minimized. You need to be responsive to your company's bottom-line needs. You may need to trade future growth for present performance (or vice versa). All of those responsibilities will keep you hopping, but if you learn to enjoy the risk of people building, you'll ease your stress.

Deputize. Find key people to entrust with parts of your responsibility. Let them deal with the problems that have been bothering you. Sometimes bosses insist on approving every decision. This usually hampers an organization's growth and puts unnecessary pressure on the boss. If you find the right people to take some responsibility, that should give you less to worry about—and it should help the whole operation. (Note: In the short run, you may have more to worry about as you train them to take responsibility, but it should pay off later.)

Give up your responsibility. If leadership is filling you with too much stress, maybe you're just not cut out for it. That's okay. Our society has this idea that your worth is determined by your place on the business ladder, but that's simply not true. Many excellent workers have found their niche: doing their work but not leading others. Unfortunately, many businesses operate on a "Peter Principle," where people rise to their level of incompetence. Whenever they do a job well, they're promoted out of it—until they stop doing well, and then they stay put. If you've been promoted into leadership and it's causing you an unhealthy amount of stress, you might want to step back down to the position where you were doing so well before getting promoted. It's a gutsy move, but it might save your life.

Cash out. Taking that tactic to the next level, you could leave your business entirely, grab your savings, and move to the mountains to sell maple syrup. Trend-watcher Faith Popcorn recognized this as a major trend in the mid-nineties, as business executives got fed up with the rat race: "Working women and men, questioning the intrinsic value of a high-powered career, are opting for more fulfillment in a simpler way of living."[4] Sure, it's a major move, which could create a lot more stress for you as you're getting set up. And of course it's hard to cash out if you don't have much cash.

Get support. We keep thinking of the stay-at-home mom, stressed from the responsibility of caring for young children. When the stress gets too tough, she needs to get help from her husband, her mom, her neighbors, anyone! She shouldn't have to go it alone. When the burden of responsibility is too heavy, share the load. If you're a teacher overwhelmed with the responsibility of an unruly class, call out for support from your principal, other teachers, teachers' aides, parents, or the kids themselves. If you're in business, let your boss, colleagues, or employees know the help you need. It's not a sign of weakness; it's a tactic for survival.

8. Do you find your coworkers difficult to work with?

WHEN YOUR COWORKERS ARE GOOD, YOUR JOB CAN BE VERY, VERY good. When they're bad, it's horrid. Think about it: If you're married, you probably spend more waking hours with your coworkers than you do with your spouse. Yet we're forced to spend time with the people we work with, like 'em or not. Sometimes we're lucky and we forge fine friendships. Sometimes we lose out.

Randy's first job as a teenager was flipping burgers at Hardee's. It was hot and greasy and hard to go to work when his friends were playing ball; but the worst part of the job was John. This guy was the boss of the back line, and he let everyone know it. John wasn't a manager or anything, he'd just been charbroiling beef patties longer than anyone else, and that made him the supreme ruler of the universe. He knew everything about everything, and he criticized everyone else. As the new guy, Randy got picked on regularly. None of the other burger flippers would stand up to John, fearing that they'd be his next target. Randy lasted six weeks, then quit.

In the following weeks, a funny thing happened. Several of Randy's friends started working at that same Hardee's. They'd come to school and talk about what a great time they'd had at work the night before. Then they got a few more friends to work there. Soon six of Randy's buddies were working there—and loving it! Randy almost wished he hadn't quit.

What about John? Oh, he was still there, but no one paid much attention to him. They had their own friendships, and so they stood up for one another when John started to attack.

In the workplace, one person can poison the atmosphere. A supportive group can make it a place of growth and joy. The inevitable stress in the workplace can be shared and transformed with the right group of people—or it can be intensified with the wrong group of people.

Many years after the Hardee's debacle, Randy worked five years for a publishing company that was losing money. There was desperation throughout the office as people tried to save the sinking ship. That stress could have caused conflict, but instead it bonded the staff. They supported one another, prayed for one another, and learned to laugh and cry with one another as the situation worsened. Eventually, the publishing enterprise folded and the people went their separate ways, but the relationships endured.

You may have experienced similar bonding in some work situations. Or maybe you've had to work with certain people you just can't stand. In those cases, the stress of daily work can magnify minor annoyances. A person's tone of voice or innocent habit can start to grate on you, until you can't bear the thought of working one more day with that jerk. But of course you have to.

Attitude can be a huge problem. If a person seems proud, as if she considers herself better than everyone else, she'll ruffle some feathers. The know-it-all practices a variation of that theme. A person who is always complaining about the company can soon lose friends; so can the one who complains about all the circumstances of his own life. On the other hand, the company cheerleader will rub some people the wrong way, as will the perennial "yes man." People who are emotionally needy, or apologizing all the time, will see people drift away after a while.

Religious or political opinions can cause battle lines to form. If a coworker is outspoken about these views, some will agree, others won't. Some workplaces can maintain a healthy debate about the issues, in which both sides agree to disagree, but others can become rancorous.

Personal habits may seem innocuous, but when you're watching a person chew with his mouth open for the 250th time that year, you have a right to protest. Nose-picking, belching, or bad breath just gross you out. Some people just won't clean up the kitchen after themselves. Others pry into your conversations or interrupt you. Some talk too loud or too often. If you saw the person once a month, you'd shrug it off — not worth worrying about. But day after day of the same old thing is like water torture.

Personality style can win friends or make enemies. Various tests have designated certain types of people. For instance, the Myers-Briggs inventory grades people along four lines — introvert/extrovert, intuitive/sensory, thinker/feeler, and judger/perceiver. If you put an Extrovert intuitive feeler perceiver copywriter in an office with an introvert sensory thinker judger accountant, they'll have their differences. If they learn to appreciate how they complement each other, they may get along well. If they just gripe about the other's shortcomings, they'll have trouble. The fact is, a business needs this alphabet soup of different personality types, but everyone has to understand that and accept the differences.

Sexual harassment may be an issue in your workplace, overtly or subtly, and it causes immense stress. We mentioned sexual harassment under question 3, but want to revisit it briefly here. Sexual harassment has many forms, and there are no rules for some forms. Attempts have been made to legislate against unwanted touches or comments, but you can't make a law against looks, and sometimes men *try* to make women feel uncomfortable in the workplace. However, harassment policies have also had a backlash, as innocent men sometimes feel nervous about expressing simple friendship with a woman at work. Can you pat her on the back as you would a male coworker? Can you joke about the sitcom you watched last night? The point is that the relationship between the sexes can add significant stress to the workplace.

Racial prejudice is another stressor that may be overt or subtle. Jokes, looks, and rude behavior based on race prejudice can make people feel uncomfortable, but biased policies of hiring or promotion hurt them professionally. Many people feel they need to work twice as hard to get a fair shake because of the color of their skin. Here again, the backlash effect has made even white males feel embattled. For many—white, black, Asian, Hispanic, male, female, whomever—prejudice has made the workplace a war zone.

What to do?

If you find your coworkers difficult to work with, it might be interesting to discover the difficulty they have in working with you. We're assuming that *they're* the problem. We haven't asked them about *your* annoying habits. So the first solution might be to examine your own working ways and make sure you're a good coworker.

Still, it's quite possible that it's not your problem at all, that you have to work with a real clinker — or at least someone who rubs you the wrong way, through no fault of your own. What can you do about that . . . short of murder?

Talk about it. Maybe you can make peace. Be honest with the other person. Say something like: "We're having a problem here, but we're going to have to work together. So we can be miserable or we can try to get along."

Disengage. Avoid the person you have a problem with as much as you can. Pay as little attention to the person as possible. If you can't avoid the person, just make a decision not to care so much about the offending behavior. Let it roll off your back. If that person has a problem, let it be his or her problem — and not yours.

Rewire your hot buttons. Consider your own response to this person. Are you having more of a problem than anyone else at work? Then maybe the offender is punching your particular "hot buttons," eliciting responses that may not be all that rational. If you figure out the true source of your discontent, you may be able to put up with the other person.

Rearrange personnel. If nothing else is working, maybe you can move to a different department or get the other person transferred. It's in your company's best interest to have employees working well together. If that can't happen, a reassignment might be the only answer. Tom saw this happen in his counseling business. Sparks were flying between two counselors in one location, so Tom moved one of them to a different office. The manager at the new office recently called Tom, saying, "I was worried when you asked me to bring in this counselor. I didn't want a problem person on staff here. But it turns out she's one of our best counselors." Sometimes it's just a clash of personalities — nothing that a little distance can't cure.

Appreciate diversity. Look for the good things in the person you can't stand. Identify the ways that he or she is different from you and consider how you might grow through your exposure to those differences. If you're a liberal, maybe you need to hear those conservative views. If you're an introvert, maybe you can learn from this extrovert. Tom learned to appreciate diversity when he was on a committee that worked well together — except for Sandi.

She regularly slowed everyone down with her "yeah, but" comments. After sensing that her input wasn't appreciated, Sandi resigned from the committee, and the group became more productive. But soon they made a quick decision that alienated the rest of the company. If only Sandi were still there, she could have slowed them down enough to see the error of their ways.

See the angels. There's an ancient Hebrew tradition that suggests angels appear to us sometimes in human guise. So imagine for a moment that this problem coworker is really an angel, sent by God for your benefit. To teach you something? To develop your patience? To enhance your compassion? You figure it out.

Kill them with kindness. The ancient Christian tradition of "turning the other cheek" may be appropriate here. Return good for evil and see what happens. Sometimes a selfless act will defuse the tension and convince the other person to drop his or her defenses, making way for a friendship (or at least a peaceful coexistence).

PART THREE

Relational Stress

RELATIONSHIPS are the best things in life. Relationships are the worst things in life. Sometimes on the same day.

In our growing collection of stress-causers, you can count on your closest relationship to cause greater stress than anything else.

Wait a second! Didn't we just say that about work? Not exactly. Work stress is more *common*—just about everyone who works experiences some work-related stress. But relationship-based stress is more debilitating. When people seek counseling, it's usually about a relationship, not about a job.

Most people expect a certain amount of stress at work. But at home, they expect a supportive relationship. Many people have relationships like that, with precious people who get them through the tough times with love and care. But when a person's primary relationship (in most cases, one's marriage) *adds* stress rather than easing it, then there's no place to find relief. You leave the frying pan of your daily work and commute to the raging fire of your home situation.

All relationships have ups and downs. You will go through stressful periods in your closest connections. But the dark night of stress brightens into the dawn of renewed support. You come through the hard times into very good times together. At least you're supposed to.

When you don't—now that's a problem. If you get stuck in conflict, your relationship becomes a stress environment. The whole fabric of your life gets frayed. Day after day, month after month, you're on edge. There's no escaping it. Your whole existence is wrapped up with this person who's driving you mad.

9. How much stress do you experience in your primary relationship?

THIS IS ANOTHER CANOPY QUESTION, DESIGNED TO LET YOU TAKE an overview of the situation before breaking it down. Ideally, your response here should be approximately the average score for the rest of this section. If you've got a lot of 4s and 5s in questions 10 to 15, but question 9 gets a 2 or 3, this relationship is more stressful than you realize. Perhaps you've grown used to the constant pressure. If question 9 has a 4 or 5 but everything else in this section is 1 to 3, then the survey probably missed something. Obviously your relationship is causing you stress, but it's not based on instability, threat, value, dissatisfaction, communication, or conflict. There are other possible stressors in a relationship.

We're talking about your *primary* relationship. If you're married, it's your spouse. If you have a steady boyfriend or girlfriend, that's who it is. Perhaps you have a roommate who's closest to you, or a coworker, or a parent, or a child. It's even possible to group several people into this "primary" relationship. A single mom with three kids would have a primary relationship with all three. A post-college person living with Mom and Dad could have a primary relationship with both of them.

We decided to focus on the primary relationship rather than relationships in general because we want you to be specific in your thinking. You need to pin down the precise feelings that cause you stress. And in most cases the primary relationship creates immensely more stress (or stress relief) than secondary relationships.

However, sometimes a secondary person will create great stress. We think of our friends Mark and Jill, who have an autistic boy. Their relationship with each other is fine, but raising their son is a full-time job. Their lives revolve around him, and they get little rest. We would advise them (and others like them) to take the test a second time, considering their son their primary relationship. (In terms of stress, he really is.)

10. How unstable do you feel in your relationship, such as the other person being unpredictable, moody, or volatile?

JIM LIVED WITH HIS FATHER, AND HE NEVER KNEW WHAT TO EXPECT. Dad could come home happy or angry, and Jim had to deal with it. If Jim's father was a little bit drunk, he was pretty harmless. If he was very drunk, watch out. If he wasn't drunk yet, he was even worse. To coexist with this man, Jim had to learn to anticipate these mood swings.

That's stressful. Millions of children of alcoholics will tell you the same story. You ride a roller coaster with a substance abuser. Their addiction becomes the pattern of your life. It runs everything. You have no certainty about anything. You're always on edge.

Any close relationship, any *family*, is like a mobile. Remember those hanging artworks you made out of coat hangers and pipe cleaners in second grade? Knock one piece of a mobile, and the whole thing starts moving. It's all interconnected. Each piece is balanced in relation to the other pieces. In a family, one volatile member may throw the whole family into chaos. In a marriage, it's sure to happen: Your spouse's wild mood swings will get you swinging too.

Sandy had been dating Don for several months when he started to get weird. Maybe he was always weird, but she was just blinded by love. Anyway, as they got closer, he started to blow up over the silliest things—a word she used, something she wore, not being ready the moment he knocked on her door. "I guess you just don't care about me," he'd say, and he'd pout or whine or yell at her. She was in love, so she put up with this nonsense for quite a while, but she soon found that the relationship was wearing her down. She could never relax with Don. She always worried about when she would offend him next, and how he would respond.

Sometimes people are attracted to unpredictability. Moody souls seem mysterious, fascinating puzzles to solve. Erratic behavior seems passionate, inspired, on the edge. Even addictive tendencies can carry the lure of flirting with danger for some people. But that act gets old. You need some peace and safety from your closest relationships, not just adventure. After the hundredth hateful, screeching, thrashing, spine-tingling, hair-pulling episode, you tend to get a bit stressed out.

Love is blind, they say. And you may be hopelessly in love with a person whose unpredictability is driving you crazy. Except you may not realize what's going on. You may consider the endless love-hate cycle to be normal. You may think it's your fault (at least that's what your significant other keeps saying). You may be taking personal responsibility for "curing" him or her of those awful bad moods. Well, good luck.

In our book on addictive relationships, *Victim of Love?*, we wrote: "Healthy relationships are a lot like mountain climbing— anything but easy. . . . Unhealthy relationships are like whirlpools. The love-hate cycle goes around and around with no real advancement. Ultimately, the relationship goes down the drain."[5]

Where is your relationship going—up the mountain or down the drain? As you try to deal with the other person's moods, do you see any progress? Or are you just fighting the same battles over and over? Those are the questions you'll have to consider as you try to change this particular stress environment.

What to do?

You might be saying, "Wait! This person isn't totally crazy, just . . . *creative*." Good point. While volatility is a mark of many addictions, as well as other problems such as depression or bipolar disorder, a lot of fairly normal people have certain amounts of unpredictability. They *do* cause stress for the people around them, but that doesn't mean their relationships are "going down the drain." With this in mind, we present a broad range of prescriptions, from casual to serious.

Know what to expect. Of course it's hard to predict an unpredictable person, but you can try. Study the mood swings and try to anticipate triggers. Certain times of day? Certain places? Certain activities? Certain other people? You may quickly figure out that your husband is going to be sullen every Sunday after you dine with his parents. You may discern that your wife gets jealous after you go out dancing. Eventually you may be able to remove the triggers, but at least for now you know what's coming.

Call ahead. If you're leaving work and you want to prepare yourself for what you'll find at home, make a call. Take a reading of the situation.

Find your own balance. You can't count on this person to be a rock of stability. And you can't judge yourself by that person's standards. You have to know who you are and what you need in life. What makes you happy? What fulfills you? Where are your talents? Who are your friends? If you establish yourself as an independent person, you can let the other person be wacky and it won't affect you as much.

Get some distance. Don't let your life revolve around this person. When he or she becomes unstable, get out of there. Maybe not forever, maybe just for the afternoon. But if you can't deal with that behavior, don't! Imagine the other person and yourself on a seesaw. He or she is clowning around, bouncing up and down, taking you for a ride that's fun for a while but sometimes it hurts. Now move back on the seesaw, away from the other person. According to the laws of leverage, you now carry more weight. The other person's antics won't move you around so much.

Find other friends. A relationship with a volatile person can become all-consuming. You can lose your other friends. (Sometimes moody people get jealous and try to get you to turn your back on other friends.) But you need perspective, you need support, and you need stress relief. Your primary relationship isn't giving you this, so get it from your friends. Give them permission to take care of you, especially if you're going through tough times.

Make some rules. If the volatility of the person you have a primary relationship with is seriously ruining your life, you need to set some boundaries and stick with them. "If you do this, I will do this." This person may protest that he or she has no control over moods and feelings. Fine, but for your own protection, emotional and otherwise, you need to set firm guidelines: "If you yell at me in public, we're going home immediately. If you start pouting, I'll ignore you. If you ever hit me, I'm moving out. Maybe you don't have control, but I do—and these are the rules."

Get counseling. If this is a serious problem, this book isn't going to fix it. You and the other person need to see a counselor. If he or she refuses, go alone. A good counselor will learn the specifics of your situation and offer effective treatment. (Volatility sometimes stems from a biological imbalance that can be treated. If addiction is behind this, you definitely need expert help. If it's "just" a personality conflict, then some behavior-based coaching may do the trick.)

Get out. In cases of violence, addiction, or severe emotional abuse, we urge people to protect themselves by moving away from the abuser. If the relationship isn't a marriage, put an end to the relationship immediately. Don't ease out. Don't do it next Wednesday. Don't have one more little talk. Get out—now! If you are married to the abuser, we don't recommend immediate divorce, but separation may be necessary. For your safety and that of any children involved—and possibly to shake some sense into the abuser—leave the premises. Find a friend, a shelter, or a church to put you up while you sort things out. Such a move may increase your stress in the short term, but it begins to build a less stressful relationship environment.

11. How threatened do you feel that your primary relationship could experience a breakup?

"IF YOU GO TO THAT MEETING, I WON'T BE HERE WHEN YOU GET BACK."
Marilyn was always threatening to leave her husband, Ben. It started the first week they were married. A high-powered executive, Ben was madly in love with Marilyn, and terrified that she would actually make good on the threat. He couldn't imagine life without her.

So, for twenty years she held the reins, and Ben lived in fear. At work, he could make decisions affecting hundreds of employees. He ran a multi-million dollar operation. But Marilyn held power over him. She had him convinced that he needed her more than she needed him. If he persisted in doing something she didn't like, she was out of there, or so she said. Over time, this debilitated Ben. He became weak and indecisive, even at work. "I feel like there's a sword of Damocles dangling over my neck," he said once. He never knew when his life with Marilyn would be over.

It finally happened after twenty years of marriage. She left him. Ben was distraught for a while, but then he picked up the pieces. Suddenly he was free of the fear that had enslaved him, free of the stress of uncertainty.

When people can't count on the future of a relationship, they often feel great anxiety—as Ben did. Sometimes this feeling of uncertainty comes from an imagined threat. This person has never even thought of breaking up with you, but you worry that it's going to happen anyway. This is common among people with low self-esteem. "Once he learns what I'm really like, it's all over." We also see this sentiment among children of divorce. Having been hurt by abandonment while growing up, they wait for it to happen again. They lack models of long-term commitment, so their relationships are tentative. If such people aren't constantly affirmed, they worry that the relationship is doomed. Often these unfounded fears become self-fulfilling prophecies, as the insecure person either breaks up the relationship first or becomes impossible to stay with.

But sometimes the threat is real. As with Marilyn and Ben, one person can use the threat of breakup as a weapon to get his or her way. Or maybe the relationship has begun to disintegrate, and the possibility of breakup is an ongoing reality. One person may suspect that the other is losing interest (or having an affair), and thus have a valid fear that a breakup is imminent.

Sometimes the threat comes from your side. That is, *you're* losing interest in the relationship, and it's just a matter of time before it's over. This tends to be a less stressful situation, because you're more in control. But it's still tough to make the move. "Should I go or should I stay?" That uncertainty can weigh on someone for months or years before the decision is finally made.

The stress of relational uncertainty may be major or minor, depending on the depth of the relationship and the intensity of the feelings. Married people who worry about an impending divorce are looking at a major upheaval, far more than those who have recently started dating. Those in casual relationships often wonder how casual they are—"Where do we stand?"—but that anxiety hardly compares with fears about divorce. Yet in any case, major or minor, real or imagined, insecurity and uncertainty can add to your stress level.

What to do?

The key to undoing the stress of insecurity is to find some security, either within the relationship or apart from it. There are various techniques to shore up a shaky relationship, but you might also try to prepare yourself for it to end. First you'll need to make a fair assessment of the threat you feel. What are the chances of a breakup? If they're, in fact, small, then you need to find ways to remind yourself of that. Work at feeling more secure, because you really are. If you're facing a substantial, but not overwhelming, chance of a breakup, then get busy at improving the chances that you'll stay together. If the breakup is inevitable, then start reinvesting your emotional resources, so you won't be so devastated when the end comes.

Communicate. On a regular basis, ask each other, "How are we doing? How can we do better?" If you're feeling insecure, say so . . . and say why. If you need more affirmation, ask for it. The best cure for the fear of the unknown is information, so keep talking with each other. Once you start communicating, you may find that the threat of breakup diminishes considerably.

Expose your demons. Your insecurity may come from your own background. Did your parents break up? Did a previous relationship crash and burn? Or do you just feel unworthy of lasting love? Many of us have histories that haunt us. Whatever your personal reasons for insecurity, talk them through. The other person in your primary relationship needs to know where you're coming from, so he or she won't accidentally trip your fears.

See a counselor. Professionals can help with your demon-exposing. In fact, counselors can help you deal with any threat to your relationship, whatever the cause. That's what they do. Some people shy away from professional counseling, seeing it as a last resort—"Couples only get help when they're in real trouble." Well, maybe that's why they get in real trouble, because they don't get help early enough. If you're troubled by the threat of a breakup, that's reason enough to see a counselor. He or she may be able to help you find peace with the past and plan workable ways of living in the present.

Disarm. If, like Marilyn in our story, the other person in your relationship uses the threat of a breakup as a weapon, you've got to get that to stop. Try some "arms limitation talks," where you explain how insecure that makes you feel. If the person persists, and if you have the guts, you might try calling his or her bluff. It's usually an empty threat, and if it stops working on you, its use will stop.

Evaluate your relationship. Is it worth the stress? If you're married, obviously that's a commitment you need to fight for. But if you're not married, and if the other person is yanking you around with this threat of breakup, playing on your feelings of insecurity, what are you still doing in that relationship?

Play the worst-case game. Get very somber for a few minutes and imagine that you get what you're afraid of—a breakup. How would you handle that? Be specific in visualizing how you would pick up the pieces. The good news is that eventually you'll be fine. It may take a year or two of grieving, but life will go on.

If a breakup is a strong possibility, you must prepare for it. You need to see the possibility of life without the other person.

Weave your safety net. Develop strong friendships apart from this primary relationship. You'll need them for support if you go through a breakup, but they can also help you evaluate your fears.

Make your decision. Remember that lack of control is a major component of unhealthy stress. But what if instead of waiting for your boyfriend to propose (or your girlfriend to accept), you set a deadline. Instead of waiting for your spouse to leave you, come up with a strong plan for staying together—going to counseling, working on specific problems.

12. How valued or understood do you feel in your relationship?

RUTH HAS ALWAYS BEEN ENTHRALLED BY DANIEL. CREATIVE, PAS-sionate, intelligent, he was her dream date, and now they've been dating for several years. Daniel's always working on some big project, advancing his career, or seeking his own personal development. Every so often he broods over events from his past, dysfunctional episodes from his family life. Ruth is always there to hold him, comfort him, nurture him, applaud him, urge him on. She has always counted herself fortunate to have a part in his amazing life.

Until recently.

One evening Ruth met Daniel for dinner with great news to share. She had received a great review at work and would be getting a promotion and raise within three months. Ruth had often struggled at her job, not always sure she was doing well, but this was a wonderful vindication. At dinner, Daniel heard her news, nodded, and went on for half an hour about his plans to launch a new Internet Web site.

Ruth suddenly realized that this was their pattern. The relationship was all about Daniel. As long as she fawned over him and his projects, everything seemed fine, but he really didn't care much about her life. If she stopped seeing him, he'd just find another cheerleader and get on with his grand life. She's still wondering what to do about it. She has hinted that she needs more attention from him, but Daniel isn't getting the hints. He's too wrapped up in himself.

We've seen this scene played out in many relationships, even marriages. People start dating in a rush of passion, doing a million little things that say, "You are important to me." He opens doors for her. She calls him at work. He brings flowers. She laughs at his dumb jokes. He goes to the ballet with her. She watches ball games with him.

There's a period of discovery in which the two begin to understand each other. You see such couples in quiet cafes, leaning forward across the table, drinking in every word along with their cappuccino. In that period, everything about the other person is new and fascinating. "So you cheated on your college boards? How enterprising!" "So you tortured mice as a child? How spirited!" We feel that we can share ourselves completely with the other person and be accepted for who we are.

Then it all begins to fade. You stop looking at each other. If you venture out to a café, you're leaning back, watching the folk singer. You've heard all the other person's jokes three times, and they were never funny to begin with. You've learned all you care to know about him or her, and you wonder how you overlooked all those glaring faults.

Chances are, that person is feeling the same way about you. The unconditional acceptance you both offered and received has now become conditional. You both feel hurt, cheated, and rejected. You pull back to protect yourself. Why should you pretend to be better than you are? "No more dining out; I'm really a pizza-and-beer guy." "This is how I really look in the morning without makeup—deal with it."

Just as a two-year-old tests the extent of a parent's love and discipline by acting out, couples often test the extent of each other's acceptance a few years into the relationship. Can I be my absolute worst and still be valued? Sadly, the answer is often no.

In good relationships, the individuals ease back into a healthy give and take. They've been completely giving and they've been completely taking, and now they enter real-life negotiations. They learn to value each other in reality, to understand and accept who the person really is, with good and bad points in balance.

But sometimes relationships get stuck in the bad cycle. The individuals involved hurt each other badly, and they never reestablish trust. Or both get so used to taking, it's hard to learn giving again. Or, as in the case of Ruth and Daniel, one keeps giving and the other keeps taking, so the relationship is out of balance.

In any case, people can find themselves undervalued in a relationship. Stress comes from their feelings of anger, of betrayal, of longing for the acceptance that was promised. And all the time there's a pulling down of self-esteem. If the person who knows you best doesn't appreciate you, what good are you? That drumbeat of disapproval makes it hard to accomplish anything.

What to do?

As with several of these test questions, you have several approaches to choose from. First, address the reality of the situation. If you don't feel valued or understood, maybe you aren't. How can you put more appreciation and understanding in your relationship? Second, address the feelings. Perhaps the appreciation is there, but you're just not getting it. Can you find ways to feel more appreciated in your primary relationship? Finally, work on your stress. Maybe you really aren't appreciated in this relationship and your feelings are valid. Can you find ways to keep those feelings from creating stress?

Make a love connection. Often couples drift apart through neglect. They just don't take time to see each other, to pay attention, to talk. It's hard to find time in the schedule just to be together, but it's crucial. So work at this. Book a time for each other, at least one hour a week, preferably more.

Go on a date. If you're married, you may have forgotten how to date. This might be fun to rediscover. Make plans in advance for dinner and a show. Dress up for it. The point is: you both need to remember what it was like to make the other feel important.

Practice listening. When couples get accustomed to each other, they stop listening. They think they've heard the whole song before, so they're already finishing each other's sentences or formulating each other's replies. Sure, this saves time, but it makes the other person feel as if he or she has nothing important to say. Slow down. Repeat what the other person says. Ask follow-up questions. Have the other person do the same for you.

Ask for what you need. We sometimes expect others to read our minds. If you're not getting the affirmation you need in a relationship, ask for it. You can phrase it in a way that doesn't sound like nagging. "I try to look nice for you, and it makes me feel good when you notice." "I'm not as sure of myself as I seem. When you say nice things to me, it really makes a big difference." Men tend to be less verbal than women, so wives and girlfriends especially need the men in their lives to give compliments.

Look for what you get. People express their appreciation in different ways. She complains, "It's our anniversary and you haven't said, 'I love you.'" He replies, "I've been hugging and kissing you all night. What else do you want?" She wants words. He offers actions. The feeling is there, but they're speaking different languages. If you're not feeling valued in your relationship, expand your vocabulary. Maybe the other person shows appreciation by serving you, touching you, or buying things for you.

Value yourself. If your relationship has soured to the point that you're not getting any affirmation, then it's up to you to find your own. That's hard to do if your spouse or friend is tearing you down at every opportunity, or if you're being ignored. It's easy to assume you have no value. That's not true. *You are important.* Within your own heart and mind, you may have to fight for that feeling.

Find others who understand. If you don't find understanding in your primary relationship, seek it elsewhere. Get a few close friends with whom you can share your soul. Discover people who will take the time to discover you. Be careful, though, about opposite-sex friendships. Affairs often start in this way—an undervalued spouse seeking understanding elsewhere—and you don't need that kind of entanglement in your life. That will only add stress. Just be wise about where you seek understanding.

13. Has your primary relationship become boring or unsatisfying?

OUR CULTURE SETS IMPOSSIBLE STANDARDS FOR US. WATCH TV AND you'll see a bevy of hunks and babes romancing each other. Read magazines and learn twenty-three tricks to keeping him happy all the time, seventeen bedroom secrets to keep your love life sizzling, or eleven ways to get her to give you what you want. Scan a billboard and see another incredibly beautiful, thin model hawking some product that promises to make you just as beautiful and thin.

The message is clear: It's supposed to be a lot better than this. By comparison, your life is drab. What are you doing wrong?

We get stressed by boring relationships because we feel a pressure to make them so much more. It's like New Year's Eve. Everyone is supposed to party like crazy on the last night of the year, right? Maybe you'd both prefer a quiet evening at home, but you don't want to be boring people, so you find something "fun" to do. You cram into some overpriced restaurant with a lot of loud, drunk people just so you can say you had a good time. You are stressed by a phantom "need." You don't really need to party, but you want to live up to the image of being "fun people."

The fact is, relationships do get boring. The passion that starts them eventually dies down. You just can't keep up that kind of energy. Boring is not necessarily bad.

Unsatisfying is another story. We enter committed relationships to get our needs met. Early in our relationships, we tend to put a lot of energy into learning and meeting each other's needs. As time goes by, we start to pay more attention to our own needs and neglect those of the other person. And sometimes the other person's needs change and we don't notice. We don't keep up with his or her growth. That's when our primary relationships fail to satisfy us.

In his classic book *His Needs, Her Needs*, Willard Harley lists the five major needs of most men and women:

Men need:
    Sexual fulfillment
    Recreational companionship
    An attractive spouse
    Domestic support
    Admiration

Women need:
    Affection
    Conversation
    Honesty and openness
    Financial support
    Family commitment[6]

We emphasize, as Harley does, that these are generalities. Your list (or your spouse's) may be different. And the lists aren't exclusive. Women also need sexual fulfillment, recreational companionship, and men need affection, conversation, and so on—just not as much. But the key point of Harley's book (and other research since then) is that men and women tend to have different needs.

Many people enter marriage (or a committed dating relationship) assuming that the other person's needs will be basically the same as their own. They follow the Golden Rule, doing for the other what they would like done for them. But that doesn't work if the other person's needs are completely different from your own! A guy can't say, "What do you mean we never go out? I just took you to a ball game!" You have to take the time to see the other person's needs.

The stress of an unsatisfying relationship comes from the feeling that there's something wrong. Maybe there is, or maybe we're just feeling pressure from our culture. Or perhaps we're feeling anger at the injustice of it all—we're working hard to meet the other's needs but no one cares about our needs. As Harley puts it, "When your basic needs go unmet, you start thinking, *This isn't right. It isn't fair.*"[7]

What to do?

Again, we're dealing with both reality and feelings. All sorts of books will tell you how to make your relationship less boring, but our purpose here is to ease the stress of your boring relationship.

Admit you're bored. If your relationship is boring, you've probably settled into a certain rhythm. You're not satisfied, but you're afraid to say anything. You don't want to hurt the other person. But the best thing you can do right now is to be honest. Say, "I'm bored with this relationship. Let's change it."

Make peace with quiet. It's okay to spend some quiet evenings at home. You don't need to be constantly on the go. A little slowdown doesn't mean your relationship is on the rocks.

Challenge the machine. Hollywood and Madison Avenue are conspiring to make you feel inadequate and unsatisfied with what you have. Don't fall into this trap. *Of course* your honey doesn't look like the people on TV. Those people don't even look that good in real life. Appreciate the real qualities of what you have, and who you have.

Change your venue. G. K. Chesterton wrote, "The only way to get back [home] is to go somewhere else; and that is the real object of travel."[8] Sometimes you need to get away from it all to see where you really are. If your relationship is growing stale, take a trip. In a new setting, you may see the other person in a new light.

Change your menu. You've settled into certain patterns, haven't you? You do this every Monday, that every Thursday. You each have your roles. You know what to expect. *Yawn.* Shake it all up. Break those patterns. Rearrange the furniture. You don't have to do exotic things, just do things in different ways.

Get new eyes. Lie on your bed, hang your head upside-down, and look at your room from this perspective. It becomes a completely different room, doesn't it? You need to get that kind of new perspective on your whole life. See the beauty in your home, in your family, in your mate. How would a visitor from another culture look at your life? Try to see everything as if you've never seen it before.

14. How difficult is the communication in your primary relationship?

SOME PEOPLE JUST DON'T TALK MUCH. IF THESE "STRONG, SILENT TYPES" are married to good conversationalists, there may be some frustration. We've heard these complaints, usually from women: "My husband doesn't have a lot to say." As we've noted before, men tend to be less verbal than women, so many marriages have an imbalance in the amount of communication desired and practiced.

But it's not always a matter of quantity. Often couples have difficulty matching up in *what* they talk about and *how* they communicate. They may talk about the weather or the kids' grades in school, but do they ever talk about their relationship? Do they say exactly what's on their minds or beat around the bush? Do they "think out loud" or mull over something in private and then deliver a pronouncement? Do they communicate in gentle, safe ways, or do they try to hurt each other with words? Are certain important subjects off limits?

People enter a relationship with different vocabularies. Take a simple phrase like "I love you." What does that mean? It can be as casual as "You're great to be with" or as serious as "You're the best thing that's ever happened to me." One person may say it freely (and want to hear it often), while another is careful with it.

People have different facility with words. Some feel very comfortable talking about their innermost emotions; others don't trust words to get their true feelings across. Or it just takes them time to formulate their phrases. Often two people will talk in different rhythms: it's hard for one to wait for the other to communicate; but it's hard for the slow one to get out the thoughts without interruption.

People have different safety zones. When talking about personal matters, some people are very touchy, others aren't. We know one couple who had a tiff over the Christmas holidays. He shrugged it off, but she was hurt by it far more than he realized. Over the next several months, she couldn't discuss it at all. They couldn't discuss *anything* about the holidays—it was too close to her pain.

People have different love languages. In his insightful book

The Five Love Languages, psychologist Gary Chapman identifies these five ways that people understand and express their love:

Words of Affirmation
Quality Time
[Giving and] Receiving Gifts
Acts of Service
Physical Touch[9]

These are like languages, he says. Some people communicate fluently in one but don't seem to recognize the others. If you want to hear words of affirmation, you may not value the fact that your spouse just washed the dishes for you (an act of service). If you communicate with physical touch, you may not want to spend hours on the phone with your boyfriend or girlfriend; but that may be just the kind of quality time that he or she needs.

Men and women tend to communicate differently. We're talking *tendencies* here—your personal patterns may be different—but researchers have found significant differences in the conversation styles of the two sexes. In our book *The Marriage Mender* (written with colleague Tom Bartlett), we summarize the data along four lines. The first is *cooperation/competition*. Whether from nature or nurture (probably both), men tend to be more competitive, women more cooperative—and this affects the way we talk and listen. "Can you help with the dishes?" is a request for a woman, but a challenge for a man. A second continuum is *exclusive/inclusive*. Men tend to be more individualistic. While women talk about *us*, men talk about *me*. A third difference is *feelings/facts*. Possibly due to the wiring between the brain hemispheres, women tend to be better at communicating emotions. Men stick with "just the facts, ma'am." Related to that is the *intuition/information* difference. Women tend to read extra cues in a conversation—tone of voice, body language, eye focus—while men usually concentrate on the words. He says, "I told you I wanted to go!" She responds, "Yes, but you weren't excited about it." She's reading more into a conversation than he is.[10]

Whether they stem from different vocabularies, different safety zones, or different "love languages," communication problems in a relationship can create frustration. Bad communication can cause misunderstandings that mess up your life in practical ways. You show up at three, the other person at four—that's a communication mixup. But deeper stress comes from the sense that the other person just doesn't get it, doesn't understand you, doesn't share your agenda for the relationship.

What to do?

In rare cases, communication problems are intentional. That is, one person doesn't *want* to communicate, and this drives the other one up the wall. Usually, however, the problems come from an *inability* to communicate. Somehow the messages aren't getting through. If you both commit yourselves to changing your patterns of speaking and listening, your lack of communication can be remedied.

Book your communication time in advance. Often the communication in a relationship dies from neglect. Each of you is doing a million different things, and you hardly see each other. If your schedules take you everywhere else, you need to be intentional about getting together to talk. Put it on the calendar, find a place where you won't be interrupted, and set a simple agenda. That agenda could be along the lines of "How are we doing?" or "What could I do better for you?" Or maybe it's just "How's work going for you these days?" or "What are your goals for the next year?"

Practice active listening. Your communication will improve if you learn to listen better. There are basic rules: don't interrupt; don't formulate your response before you hear all the other person is saying; don't let emotions overwhelm the message. These seem like common sense, but they're tougher than they sound. A good exercise is called "active listening," where you repeat what you hear the other person saying. Ask the person, "Is that what you're saying?" Don't respond until you're sure you got the message straight. It takes longer to converse this way, but is that so bad? At least it ensures that you're paying full attention to what the other person is trying to say.

Set the ground rules. Speaking of emotions, they can often turn communication into a battle. Who wins? Are you right or am I? If you hurt me, I'll hurt you twice as much. Some people are skilled in attacking others with words. They know just how to insult or offend the other person. That, of course, results in a defensive attitude, in which a person brags or counterattacks. All of this game-playing sabotages good communication. How can you get any information across when you're constantly attacking or defending? If certain "hot buttons" trigger a highly emotional response, stay away from them.

Commit yourselves to safety. You must promise that both of you can speak freely. Safety starts with *respect*, the understanding that the other person has something valuable to say. It also engenders a win-win spirit, the assumption that both of you should gain something through the conversation. If one of you comes out a loser, then the relationship itself loses too.

Agree to disagree. You won't always see eye to eye. Problems occur when one person forces an issue, insisting that the other change his or her mind. Accept the fact that complete agreement is unlikely, if not impossible. You don't have to convert the other person to your way of thinking. If there's a practical matter involved—how you discipline the kids, where you live, or how you spend money—work at finding a compromise you can both live with.

Understand conversation styles. Don't just learn the generalities of how men and women communicate; study how your partner does it. He or she may not fit the mold. Talk about facts and feelings, competition and cooperation, and so on. You don't need to adopt the same style, but at least get a working knowledge of the other person's way of speaking.

Learn the other person's love language. Take some time to consider the differences in the way love is expressed. Are you a gift giver, complimenter, servant, toucher, or time spender? How do you like to receive love? What does the other person like? As you learn to show love in the way he or she prefers, you'll hop over a number of communication hurdles.

Write a letter. When people speak in different rhythms, interruption can be a problem. One of you struggles to find the right words while the other grows impatient and finishes the sentences—or stops listening. If you're frustrated because you can't seem to get a word in edgewise, write down your feelings. That way, the other person will have it all there, and can't interrupt.

15. How much conflict do you experience in your primary relationship?

AL AND JUDY WERE BOTH CORPORATE EXECUTIVES WITH BUSY, BUSY lives. They met on the job and zoomed into a relationship that was mostly physical. Soon they conducted their own personal merger . . . marriage. But their schedules were still horrible. When they weren't separately jetting around the world, they were working fourteen-hour days.

In their leadership responsibilities at work, they could bark out orders and get things done. It wasn't that easy at home. They were constantly arguing, over the pettiest things.

"I thought you were going to walk the dog."

"Only if I got home first. But I had to work late."

"You worked late intentionally so you wouldn't have to walk the dog."

"Did not!"

When they came to Tom for counseling, they were close to divorce, even though they'd only been married a year. And even in Tom's office, they'd yell at each other.

Obviously, they were both dealing with a lot of stress in their jobs. You can't keep up fourteen-hour days for long without feeling a bit frazzled. But work was a picnic compared to the conflict they faced at home. They needed their relationship to ease their stressful lives, but instead it was like throwing gasoline on a fire.

Al and Judy aren't alone here. Relational conflict creates enormous stress in many people's lives. We see it among couples who've been married for many years. Along the way they've dug their battle trenches, and now every issue is a world war. We also see it among couples in years two through five of a marriage—a period we call "energized conflict." The honeymoon is over, the lofty expectations of an idyllic life together have been shattered, and now both partners are fighting to gain the upper hand in their marriage. (With Al and Judy that period came a bit early.)

If they learn to work through their conflict, find some peace, and grow into what we call a "mature love," they'll find a balance between *us* and *me*. That is, they can communicate their individual needs and work out the necessary compromises to make the relationship work, too.

Conflict can cause stress in dating relationships, too, but usually it's not as intense. Unless something else is holding the couple together (addiction, sex, kids, family pressure), conflict will drive them apart. The same can be said for roommate or best-friend relationships. If your "primary relationship" is with a family member, that's a bond that can resist a good deal of conflict—which means you'll have to stay in the relationship and deal with the stress of conflict.

Any close relationship will have some conflict, but we're talking about a pattern of conflict that's hard to escape. In conflict-riddled relationships, each person views the other as the enemy. It becomes very important to win each battle, and to make the other person lose.

With Al and Judy, the key to restoring their relationship was to shift the battle lines. They had to stop seeing each other as the enemy. Their busy schedules were the real foe. If they could ease up on their workloads, they'd both be able to give a little in their relationship. That would ease the tension.

A relationship in conflict is often like a tug of war. Both people are pulling with all their might. They can't give in, or else they'll lose. That constant tension becomes normal for them. They don't know any other way to live except to fight the other person. But if even one of them stops pulling, it changes everything. If they decide to fight their problems instead of each other, if they pick up the same end of the rope and join forces against a common foe, they can heal many of their wounds.

Al and Judy were doers. They knew how to tackle problems on the job, and they brought that same resolve to their marriage. Once they "let go of the rope," understanding that it was senseless to fight each other, they could make some real progress.

They agreed to work only twelve hours a day (only!), coming home at six rather than eight. This was a hard choice for them. Both had assumed that work would always have first place in their lives. But now they had another priority, their relationship. They set some rules about their schedules, and they doggedly stuck to them.

They also set aside one evening a week as "date night," being sure to spend at least that much quality time together. And they developed a common hobby, sailing. With their salaries, they could easily buy a nice sailboat, and they began learning the ropes together. Soon their relationship was sailing along nicely too.

What to do?

Conflict is inherently stressful, so if you're stressed out by the conflict in your relationship, you just have to stop fighting. If you don't mind losing a few battles, you may just win back your relationship.

Shift your target. Find the real enemy. Maybe your schedule is burdening you. Maybe there are outside pressures. Maybe one or both of you are trying to fulfill impossible expectations. Maybe you've entered marriage expecting unreasonable things of your mate. In any case, try to see the two of you on the same side of the battle.

Lose one for the gipper. That's right, throw a fight. Let the other person win. Somehow you have to break your pattern of conflict. So, next time you have an argument, simply say, "You're right."

Pick your battles. There are some issues worth fighting for, but there are many insignificant ones. It seems to us that the petty fights are more damaging. Let go of the silly little things—what's for dinner, what TV show you're going to watch, and so on—so you'll be able to talk more reasonably about the major things.

Learn creative negotiation. The old style of business transactions was win-lose. Both parties tried to gain the advantage. But as long as both sides are trying to win at the expense of the other, they both lose. The new style is win-win. How can both parties come out ahead? That's the strategy you need to assume in your relationship negotiations. Both of you have to decide to give something and take something, and you need to divvy things up fairly. You might trade one decision for another (you drive the kids, I'll do the dishes); go half and half (we'll spend half the money on home improvements and half on new clothes); or come up with a third course of action you can both agree on (we'll paint the bedroom, not blue, not red, but green).

Give 55 percent. Even when couples try to be fair with each other, they can remain in conflict. Why? They may be trying to divide everything 50-50, but everyone tends to overestimate what they're giving and underestimate what they're getting. So you think you're giving 50 percent when you're only giving 45. Of course, the other person is making the same mistake. So that's where most of the conflict occurs in a relationship, "between the 45s." You both think you're being fair and the other's being unreasonable. What if you both aimed at 55 percent, giving a little more than you get? Then even with the fudge factor, you meet at 50-50.

Have fun together. Some couples get so embattled that they forget what brought them together to begin with. Learn to date again. Develop a common hobby. Do together the things you have fun doing. Then you'll build a collection of happy memories about the other person. This "recreational companionship," as Willard Harley calls it, "is one of the easiest ways for married couples to build good feelings about each other. All they need to do is to be with each other while they're having a good time."[11]

See a counselor. Sometimes your conflicts get so bad that you need outside help. Rather than drawing family or friends into your mess (they may choose sides and make things worse), go to a professional. A good counselor should help you see your relationship with new eyes and assist you in finding practical solutions.

---

16. How much stress do you experience in your secondary relationships, such as with a close friend or a family member?

NATE AND STEVE HAD BEEN BEST FRIENDS FOR YEARS. THEY WENT to ball games together, their families partied together, their kids grew up together. A high-ranking corporate executive, Steve was a bit fast-paced for Nate. Steve made more money, spent more money, and liked the finer things in life. He also cheated on his wife. By contrast, Nate was a low-key guy, not flashy at all, but a loyal friend. When Steve got divorced, Nate stuck with him. Steve often commented that he needed a friend like Nate to keep him grounded.

The friendship continued as Steve remarried, and divorced again. Nate would listen patiently as Steve complained about having to pay two alimonies. Surely he didn't need to be reminded that he had brought it on himself. No, Nate continued to be supportive.

Then there was a silly misunderstanding. Nate and his wife were going to meet Steve for dinner, and they were a bit late. Steve was waiting at the bar when they came, but they didn't see him, so they went ahead with dinner. Steve finished his drink and went home. A silly mix up, but Steve was upset about it. In their ensuing conversations, he made it clear that he wanted to end his friendship with Nate and his wife. "He ran out of wives to divorce," Nate quipped, "so now he's divorcing his friends."

That comment was uncannily accurate. This "breakup" hit Nate hard. It *was* like a divorce. For several weeks he tried to contact Steve, but Steve wasn't responding. It was over. This was a stressful time for Nate. He couldn't watch a football game without missing his friend. He became depressed, then angry, then depressed again.

If Nate took the Stress Test, his primary relationship would be with his wife, and there's not a lot of stress there. Yet he's feeling considerable stress from his secondary relationship with Steve. That's why we included this question, so the test would include the significant stress that comes from secondary sources.

We know many parents who are having a hard time rearing their children. The kids are unruly, rebellious, hanging with the wrong crowd. Again, the primary relationship—the marriage—may be fine, but the relationship with the child(ren) is highly stressful.

Any of the questions on the test about primary relationships can also apply to secondary relationships. You might feel unstable, insecure, or undervalued by your close friends or family members. There might be conflict or a lack of communication, or you might just be bored with the relationship. The effect of the stress in these cases depends on how important the secondary relationship is to you. You won't be too upset if a casual friend threatens never to see you again. But if it's a long-term, deep friendship like that of Nate and Steve, that would bother you a lot. If your teenage daughter says she might run away, that's calamitous.

Still, you don't expect as much from secondary relationships as you do from primary ones. If you're married, you look to your spouse for security, affirmation, and fulfillment. If you feel threatened, underappreciated, or unfulfilled in your marriage, you experience stress. It's not the same with a secondary relationship, even a close one. You may experience some pain with the breakup (or fading away) of a friendship, but it's not your only source of fulfillment.

Escapability is another factor. Again and again we've said that one way to lessen relational stress is to distance yourself from the person who's troubling you. That's pretty easy in a casual friendship: just avoid the person. But if you're dealing with a coworker or family member, you can't escape as easily. If there's a conflict, you need to deal with it, because you know you'll be sitting across from that person next Thanksgiving—or in the office Monday morning.

What to do?

If a secondary relationship is causing you stress, go back over questions 10 to 15 to determine the specific source of that stress. Then review the "What to do?" section for the applicable question(s).

How much is it worth to you? Is this secondary relationship really worth the amount of stress it's causing you? It might be best to take time off from this relationship, or at least downgrade the level of your friendship. That's tough if it's a family member or coworker, but even then you should look for ways to distance yourself from the behavior that's stressing you.

Talk about it. With some friends or family members, you can be absolutely honest. Say, "I'm dealing with a lot of stress right now, and our relationship is making it worse. Can we try not to fight so much?" (or whatever the problem is). If the person is really a friend, she'll understand.

Set boundaries. For your own health and safety, you need boundaries—otherwise you'll deplete yourself. You shouldn't feel bad about making certain rules for your relationships: not taking calls after 9 P.M.; not lending money; not seeing the person more than twice a week; not getting in the middle of other people's relationships.

Share the burden. The irony of all this is that relationships should be stress *relievers*, and often they are. But if you have a particular friend or relative who causes you stress, draw other friends into the picture. Don't be the only friend of this problem person. Get others to help you.

Increasingly, middle-aged people are experiencing the stress of caring for their elderly parents. Here, too, you should seek to share the burden as much as possible—with your siblings or children, with volunteers from church or community groups, or with professional caregivers. You can't distance yourself from this stress, but you can dilute it.

PART FOUR

Personal Stress

"WHEREVER you go, there you are."

That sounded really funny in junior high, but it's actually the basis for the next section of the Stress Test. Dealing with environmental stress, it's natural to consider work and relationships; but there's another part of your environment you can never get away from—you! Whatever stress you chronically give yourself is a constant part of your life.

A number of personal habits and lifestyle decisions appear in the Aggravator and Fitness portions of the test, but in the environment section we've included matters of self-understanding. The factors that make you who you are and the way you look at your life—these all create a sort of "personal environment" which may be stressful or not.

---

17. How secure, or confident, do you feel in your abilities?

DIANA SAT NERVOUSLY IN THE JOB INTERVIEW. A SINGLE MOM WITH three kids, she just had to make some money, so she answered an ad for a secretarial job in Tom's office. In the interview, she did everything wrong, presenting herself rather poorly.

"What skills do you have for the job?"

"Nothing much. I've just been caring for my kids, really."

"How about typing?"

"Oh, I don't think I'm very good at that."

Doubting her abilities, she was putting her worst foot forward. But Tom suspected there was more to Diana than she was letting on. He had fought a few bouts with insecurity himself, so he knew how that could mask someone's true talents. He gave Diana the job after all.

He was very glad he did. Her lack of confidence hindered her at first, but then she began to feel more secure. As she learned the job, Diana became an excellent secretary. Her typing skills were fine, and she did all her work beautifully. But her greatest strength turned out to be her people skills. She brought new business to the center just by her outgoing and vivacious spirit. She stayed there five years, then jumped to a better job, where she now earns more than Tom. Go figure.

You may know people of limited ability who make up for it with confidence. They're always trying bold new projects and trumpeting their accomplishments, even though their talent is minimal. But it's more common to see people on the other side of the spectrum. They're really quite talented, but they don't seem to know it. Their lack of confidence keeps them from using the abilities they have.

What to do?

People who lack confidence live in fear and frustration. They often find themselves underemployed because they've never taken the chance to make full use of their abilities. Then they get bored and unfulfilled in those jobs, creating even more stress.

Take wise chances. To build your confidence, you need to try something and succeed at it. That's risky. But you don't have to take crazy risks. Hedge your bets, get good advice, and try something with a good chance of success.

Form a cheering section. Gather people around you who say nice things to you and mean them. Get away from those who criticize you all the time. You need people who see your true abilities and applaud them.

Appreciate the effort. Every failure brings you a step closer to your next success. Even if you try something and fail, try to compliment yourself for the effort. A friend of ours once told us about the Kamikaze Club he belonged to in college. These ordinary guys decided to ask out all the most beautiful girls on campus—expecting to get shot down, but congratulating each other on the attempts. (To their surprise, they got quite a few dates.)

Name your villains. Where does your insecurity come from? Childhood experiences? Sibling rivalry? Critical parents or teachers? Should those factors continue to dominate your life? In preparation for our book *Becoming Your Own Best Friend*, we surveyed a number of people about self-esteem issues. We got several poignant answers:

"I was cut from the football squad. Dad called me a loser for not making it. I decided to prove him right."

"My twelve-year marriage was lonely and unfulfilling."

"I was ridiculed when I was a child, primarily because I was the youngest. No amount of praise from my family would compensate for the teasing."[12]

Whatever it was that stole your confidence, it's time to undo it. See how wrong those ancient naysayers are, and take a chance on your own abilities.

Know yourself. You're not perfect. You don't have to be. But you have some God-given abilities; learn what they are. Ask your friends, take an aptitude test, see a counselor, but start using these abilities. Get to know the stranger within you. You may find a pretty fascinating person in there.

18. How satisfied are you with your life right now?

HOW MUCH MONEY ARE YOU EARNING NOW? IF YOU THINK BACK, you can probably remember a time when you said, "If I could only earn that much money, I'd be satisfied." Now you're making that amount: Are you satisfied?

It's not just money we long for. "If I could only lose twenty pounds, then my life would be great." It might be a fine idea to lose the weight, but it's not going to bring you satisfaction.

If I could only drive that car, write that novel, marry that person, regrow my hair, buy that computer, move into that community, have kids, send my kids off to school, get that job, work for myself, retire . . . *then* I would finally be happy.

Trust us. "Then" never arrives. If you're not happy now, no car, computer, or head of hair will make you happy. Satisfaction doesn't come from what you have. It's a state of mind, an attitude of gratitude.

We're not saying you shouldn't challenge yourself. Go ahead, write that novel. But don't simmer in your dissatisfaction. That creates stress. You're always reaching for something more. You can never relax where you are.

Some dissatisfied people set up impossible expectations: "I'll make a million by the time I'm 25." Then when they find themselves working at Starbucks to pay off college loans, well, of course they're not happy.

Others are always comparing themselves with others. "Look, there's a 25-year-old starting his own Internet company! Why can't I do that?" Or maybe there's a brother or classmate who always looms ahead. Unless they get ahead of that person, they're not doing well enough.

But many dissatisfied people set reasonable goals, yet when they reach them they're *still* not happy. It's as if they're not wired for satisfaction. There always has to be some new dream of a better life out there somewhere, beyond their grasp.

What to do?

The strategy here is all mental. It's tempting to say, "Work hard to meet your goals, and then you'll have reason to be satisfied," but you can find satisfaction right where you are, on the road to wherever you're going. Accomplishment is nice, but it doesn't guarantee satisfaction.

Be content with what you have. The money you have. The body you have. The spouse you have. The job you have. It sounds trite, but count your blessings. Whenever you start wishing for something, temper it with a measure of thanks for what you already have. We've seen a lot of people with various problems, and this attitude is the most significant factor in their recovery.

Stop living for someday. Take stock of your present situation. Sometimes it's just a matter of focus. If you're always thinking about future desires, you'll ignore what you have right now. So take a few moments every day to look around you. "Stand in the place where you are," as the song goes, and recognize all the good things you already have.

Get real. That doesn't mean you can't plan for the future, but be realistic about it. Push yourself a little, but don't set impossible goals.

Get specific. Dissatisfaction can become a huge blob that creeps through your whole life. Everything disappoints you, and that's stressful. Unless you get specific, you'll never see the individual glimmers of hope. If you want to improve particular areas of your life—relationships, career, financial savings, spiritual development—then go for it. Set goals and work toward them. But don't let the blob of bitterness take over.

Unseat the judges. All sorts of people will tell you why you shouldn't be satisfied with your life. Some of them think they're doing you a favor; others are just mean. Ignore the judges. Don't let them determine whether you're doing well or not. You're the expert on your performance. Make your own decisions.

---

19. Do you have unresolved issues from your past or family of origin which affect you today?

WE ALL HAVE OUR ISSUES, AND MOST OF THEM COME FROM OUR childhood. You may be afraid of commitment because your father walked out. You may be very competitive because you had an older brother you tried to keep up with. You may not trust people because your classmates always played tricks on you.

In the last three decades, our society has learned a bit about psychology, just enough to be dangerous. We've started to blame everything on our upbringing. Every family is labeled "dysfunctional" in some way. If your family functioned perfectly, well, then you must be in denial.

But there's a basic truth here, even if many people misuse it. Many families *are* dysfunctional. We *are* affected by our upbringing. From our parents, siblings, teachers, and our playmates, we learned a great deal about who we are and how to live. Of course that will have a great effect on us throughout our lives. It doesn't diminish our responsibility to make good choices, but it does help us understand ourselves better.

Issues from the past can cause stress. They affect your attitude, contributing to your "personal environment." But they also affect your decision making, which can put you in other high-stress environments. For instance, we've encountered a number of people from dysfunctional families who had a habit of getting into abusive relationships. Issues from the past can also introduce you to various stress aggravators, such as substance abuse or other addictive behavior.

What to do?

If you have a seriously dysfunctional past, there's no quick fix. You need to commit yourself long term to undoing the damage. But if there are minor issues from your past, some simple mental discipline may be enough to ease your stress.

Get therapy. For serious and even moderate issues, you need professional help. A good counselor will help you unravel your personal history and set you on a road toward healing. We favor a solution-based approach, one that doesn't just dwell on the past but includes practical pattern setting for the future.

Do some digging. When the past is painful, we tend to bury it. You may need to go back and do some excavation. What really happened? How and when did you learn your present patterns? Talk with your parents, siblings, and old friends to get to the truth. If you're dealing with explosive issues, be careful about the emotions of your parents (and others involved). It's not about blaming, just finding answers. Note: Digging through the past may bring you more stress in the short term. You may want to wait for the right time. And if there are serious problems back there, be sure to get a counselor's help.

Debunk the voices. Most people hear voices in their heads. (Relax: You're not the only one!) The voices tell you you're no good, you can't do it, don't even try, you'll never amount to anything. The voices are wrong. They come from people in your past who never had the whole story. They couldn't possibly know what you would become. You're a much different person now, and you can prove them wrong. So go ahead: Talk back to those voices, out loud if it helps.

Take a journey of self-discovery. That was then, this is now. The good news is that you don't have to be enslaved by your past. It's a new day. Start taking stock of who you are now. What talents do you have, what friends do you have, what ideas and emotions are swimming through you? Discover and celebrate who you are now.

Practice your long division. Sometimes guilt about the past rears its ugly head, terrorizing your current life. But often those feelings are all mixed up. In our book *Becoming Your Own Best Friend*, we talked about "dividing" those feelings to get a better grasp of the truth. First, divide what you have done from what's been done to you. You may be a victim here, and not to blame at all. Second, divide who you are from what you have done. You may have done bad things, but that doesn't take away your value as a person. Finally, divide who you've been from who you will be. Maybe you've been a scoundrel, but you can change.[13]

20. Are you concerned about the future?

REMEMBER THE Y2K PROBLEM? PEOPLE WERE IN A FRENZY approaching the turn of the millennium, certain that disaster would befall the human race. Oh, there are always the doom-sayers who see Armageddon in every headline, but this time we had a genuine, computer-generated crisis! With microchips unable to read the date of 1/1/2000, surely our computer-dependent society would fold.

Well, if you're reading this book, chances are you survived. (We're writing this in 1999, so we're going out on a limb, but we think the panic is unfounded. We're guessing that there were a few Y2K-related glitches that probably created some minor problems, but life is going on.)

People were stressed about the year 2000, and before that they were stressed about the meteor supposedly headed for earth, and before that they were stressed about the Gulf War, and before that it was nuclear war, or the economy, or the oil crisis, or the creeping influence of communism. There's always something to scare you, if you let it.

The problem is, you can't do much about any of these things. Maybe build a bomb shelter, stockpile some goods, buy some Krugerrands. But the events that happen will happen whether you live in fear or not. German theologian Dietrich Bonhoeffer wrote, "The coming day, even the coming hour, are placed beyond our control. It is senseless to pretend that we can make provision because we cannot alter the circumstances of our world. Only God can take care, for it is he who rules the world."[14] Bonhoeffer was commenting on Jesus' saying: "Do not be anxious about tomorrow" (Matthew 6:34, RSV). You have to agree that there's little you can do to change world events. A certain amount of trust and acceptance is required.

People also worry about cultural trends that change the world. Conservatives fret about the sliding morals of society. Citydwellers see crime running rampant in the streets they used to walk freely. Educators bemoan the shrinking attention spans of . . . oh, who really cares? Everything seems to be going downhill and we seem powerless to stop it. There's that lack of control again, a key component of stress.

But it's not just world events that spark anxiety. Parents worry about the future of their children. Some aren't sure whether they'll have enough money to live on in the coming years. A thirty-year-old sees her first gray hair and starts thinking about aging. A sixty-year-old sees her gray-haired reflection and starts thinking about death.

Tom will never forget a woman he met at a seminar where he was speaking. Different people in the group were sharing their concerns about life—bad jobs, bad relationships—but this woman seemed to have a peace about her. She looked a bit odd, with big eyes peering out from under a big hat. As she began to speak, it became clear what was different about her.

"I'm dying of cancer," she said. "They tell me I could live for two months or two years." That explained her pallid complexion, the missing eyebrows, and there was probably little hair under that floppy hat. But the woman went on to talk about the way she lived each day in simple faith. Tom was no longer the teacher of this class. You could almost feel the gripes being lifted from everyone else's heart.

The woman had "freaked out" when she was first diagnosed, but then she set about putting her life in order, restoring relationships, and making peace with God. She couldn't control the cancer, but she could still control her life, as long as she had it. She was no longer a victim, but a victor, and she spoke with a deep serenity that touched everyone in the room.

What to do?

If you're stressed by the fear of the future, you can take two positive approaches. One is to get a more realistic perspective on the future, ruling out unreasonable fears. The second is to make peace with your reasonable fears.

Deal with probabilities, not possibilities. Learn to distinguish between probable events and improbable ones. If there's only an infinitesimal chance that some bad thing will happen to you, then don't let it trouble you. It's not worth even a nanosecond of your time.

Make reasonable preparations. If there's a probability that something bad will happen, do what you can to prepare for it. But don't go crazy. If the world's computers are in danger of freezing up, then make sure you have a few days worth of food in your pantry. But you don't need to go live in a cave or stockpile weapons.

Just say no to fear. Even after you rule out the silly fears, you'll have plenty of legitimate things to worry about. You will grow old, unless you die young. You will probably lose people you love, unless they lose you first. You will experience some pain and suffering. These are certainties; now does it help you to be afraid of them? No. Fear just makes you grow older faster, or it hastens your death. Fear just hurts you more. So choose not to focus on those negative events. Or choose to see the positive aspects of those negative events.

Get your priorities straight. Are you afraid of losing your money? How bad would that be? Should money be the most important thing in your life? What if someone broke into your house and stole some expensive things? Aren't they just things? Sometimes those moments of crisis make us appreciate the more important things in life.

Live by faith. We aren't guaranteed long life, health, or lasting relationships. We might lose any of those things in an instant. But the most serene people on this earth, like the woman at Tom's seminar, have chosen to put their trust in Someone beyond them. They don't know what the future holds, but they know Who holds the future.

PART FIVE

Community Stress

LAST year Jessica moved to the city. She'd lived all her life in a suburban area with her parents, but when they were moving away, she had to get her own place. So she found a downtown apartment ten blocks from her job.

Making her decision, she weighed the finances involved. She'd be paying high rent for a small place. Surely she could find a better deal in the suburbs, but then she'd have a longer and more expensive commute. Now she hops on a bus and gets to work in ten minutes for less than a buck. In the suburbs she'd need a car, along with all the expenses that would entail; in the city she can do without one.

What she didn't consider was the stress involved. Not just the stress of moving—that's going to cause temporary stress wherever you go—but the ongoing stress of living in the city. Safety is a constant concern. As a single woman, she has to be especially careful whenever she ventures out, especially after dark. Crowding is another problem. She may not have to fight freeway traffic, but now she's always elbow-to-elbow with other pedestrians or bus-riders. The city has a certain hectic pace that takes some getting used to. Noise is another city stressor. At all hours of the night she hears horns honking, brakes squealing, or drunks shouting from the streets below. And, while the city offers many great things within a small area, it's not as convenient as you might think. She's a stone's throw from jazz clubs and theaters, but her supermarket is ten blocks away. Without a car, she has to lug her groceries that distance, sometimes after dark. It's always an adventure.

It's no surprise that sometimes Jessica just needs to get away. The community stress of the big city can become overwhelming.

But suburban life is no picnic either. Have you ever tried to find a parking place at a mall in December? At rush hour, freeways become freezeways, as cars inch along at glacial speeds. And rush hours are lasting longer and longer. If you don't pick the right time, even driving down to the corner for a loaf of bread can put you in a jam. And perhaps there was a time when suburbs seemed safe enough to keep your doors unlocked, but no more. Kidnappings, burglaries, vandalism, and shootings are routinely reported these days even in the most comfortable communities.

So the answer is to move out to the country, right? Maybe. The pace of life is slower there, but where can you find a good deli? Or a hospital? Seriously, the same isolation that gives you peace and quiet also removes you from many of the comforts and necessities of life. That may cause you some stress.

Sure, there are plusses and minuses to any location. You'll find the kind of turf that's right for you, unless you're forced to live elsewhere because of a job or relationship. You may have a "Green Acres" marriage where he wants "farm living" and she says, "Darling, I love you, but give me Park Avenue." One of you will be out of place. In any case, you need to be aware of the different stresses involved in different communities and do what you can to counteract them.

21. How unsafe do you feel in your neighborhood?

IN THE LAST FEW YEARS, POLICE REPORT CRIME HAS BEEN ON THE decrease. But statistics don't matter much when you read newspaper accounts of murders and burglaries in your neighborhood. Crime may be officially less frequent, or less reported, but it has certainly seeped throughout our society.

Randy has been troubled lately to learn that two people he knew as children have been convicted in two separate murders. These were nice kids, suburban, middle class, not voted "most likely to be felons." But now they're killers. Make no mistake; it can happen anywhere.

What to do?

Once again, we've stoked your stress fires, rather than extinguishing them. But stress management shouldn't involve ignoring reality. You need to accept a situation and deal with it. If crime in your community troubles you, you need to evaluate the danger honestly and plan your response.

Understand the threat. Sometimes the media sensationalize crime so much that we fear it more than we have to. In the United States, there were about 13.5 million violent and property crimes committed in 1996, or one for every 20 citizens. More than half of these were larceny theft; stuff was taken but people weren't hurt. There were only 1.68 million violent crimes reported, one for every 157 citizens, but only a fraction of these were murders. There were fewer than 20,000 murders that year, meaning that your chances of being murdered were about one in 13,600. But the statistics don't say how many of those victims were involved in crime or drug use themselves. If you're clean and careful, the risk is even more remote.

Move. Of course some neighborhoods are dangerous. If you can't take the stress of living there, do what you can to move to a safer environment.

Be wise. Don't walk down the street with hundred-dollar bills hanging out of your pockets. You can take wise precautions without being paranoid. Try to be aware of the people around you, but don't fear them. Be especially careful after dark. Lock doors and windows. Invest in alarms or other anti-theft devices.

Start a safety patrol. Get to know neighbors and friends who will look out for you, as you look out for them. Join a neighborhood watch program. If you have to go out at night, ask someone else to go with you. There's safety in numbers.

Know what's most important. People are more important than property. Get that principle fixed in your head. Theft or fire or natural disaster may rob you of some stuff, but your life is much more precious.

Don't give in to terrorists. We know an elderly couple who live in a changing neighborhood. They've begun to fear the strangers who walk by their house, and so they're always fretting about locking doors, turning on lights, getting their mail before anyone steals it. They're so afraid of being robbed that they've robbed themselves of joy and peace. It's fine to take precautions, but if you're living in fear, you've already lost.

Meet the enemy. Face it—sometimes in a changing community fear is racially motivated. Whites worry when Blacks move in. Blacks worry about Asians. Asians worry about Latinos. There's always a "them" that we fear because we don't know better. Work at breaking down that wall. If a family of another race has moved in down the block, invite them to dinner. Get to know them personally, and then you won't be so worried about their "kind."

Seek shelter. If you're overwhelmed by the stress of living in an unsafe neighborhood, you need to schedule a time and place to put those worries away. Maybe you can get away from the neighborhood for a weekend once a month, camping in the country. Or after you jostle through busy city streets on your way home from work, you could sink into a relaxing bubble bath.

22. How difficult are traffic, congestion, and transportation problems for you in your community?

WE LIVE ON OPPOSITE SIDES OF PHILADELPHIA. WHENEVER WE MEET, one of us (usually Randy) has to drive through the city on one of its lovely highways. The trip takes 45 minutes, unless there's traffic. There's always traffic.

You could say the same about any metropolitan area. As businesses move out from the cities, roads get more crowded everywhere. Old roads and bridges are falling apart, requiring construction that backs up the already-congested thoroughfares.

No wonder road rage is reaching epidemic proportions. We read about drivers in Los Angeles brandishing guns in traffic jams and a famous boxer losing his cool over a fender bender. Driving is becoming a high-stress activity.

Anger is about justice. We rage when we feel we're being treated unfairly. We deserve to get from home to work in a half-hour. This stupid traffic jam is making us late, robbing us of valuable work time! That's not fair!

But what if we revised our expectations? What if we saw ourselves as horse-and-buggy people who didn't deserve to have such a wonderful machine as a car? What if we were thankful that we could drive at all, and accepted traffic tie-ups as an inevitable part of this great gift of transportation? That may sound weird, but it's the best way to tackle road rage. Reevaluate what's fair. Downgrade your sense of what you deserve. That should make it a bit easier to deal with nasty traffic.

What to do?

Sell your car—that would solve it. Well, no, we're assuming that you're going to have to keep driving through these messes. Maybe you can bypass the worst traffic situations, but the most important thing is to tame your driving stress.

Flex your schedule. See if you can bypass rush hour by going into work early or staying late. Maybe you can work at home one day a week. Employers are increasingly willing to consider such options.

Take the bus. Sure, this might add a whole new set of stressors, but you should consider alternate means of transportation.

Allow extra time. Driving stress is worst when you're running late. You have to get to the airport by five and this blasted truck in front of you is going twenty miles per hour! Well, if you left yourself an extra half-hour, you could enjoy the slower ride.

Get a cell phone. We have no desire to add technology to your life, but here's something that might help. A big problem with driving delays is communication. They're expecting you at the meeting, but you're stuck on the beltway. So call them and explain. (Try not to use the phone to work while you drive. That will add stress. But for emergencies, it will help you control the situation.)

Let jerks be jerks. Do you get mad at bad drivers? When cars pass you on the right, doing ninety, weaving through traffic, do you want to gun your engine, catch up, and box them in? Don't. It's not worth it. Let go of your desire for highway justice.

Make good time. We talk about "making good time" on a trip, but how about making it truly good? Take the scenic route, leave the stopwatch at home, enjoy the ride. Then the delays won't matter so much.

Turn your car into a haven. Have tapes on hand with relaxing music. Put a picture of someone you love on the dashboard. If you're used to sitting in traffic jams, bring some work to do.

Invent a quick refresher. Monitor your stress levels, and when you feel your temperature rising, take a few deep breaths. Or do a "progressive tensing" exercise where, starting from your feet, you tense up and relax each part of your body. Or imagine yourself in some idyllic setting. Find what works for you.

23. How isolated do you feel in your neighborhood?

RANDY WAS AT HIS SISTER'S FOR THANKSGIVING, AND THEY NEEDED more apple cider, so he volunteered to go out for some. Understand that Randy is a suburban guy, with a convenience store two blocks away from his home. But his sister lives out in the country, "over the river and through the woods." He expected this to be a quick trip down to the corner, but he drove and drove and drove, looking for a store that sold cider. He finally found a gas station mini-market, but no cider. More driving and finally there was a town with a little supermarket—but apparently too little to carry cider. Driving on to a larger town, with a larger supermarket, he finally bagged his cider. Randy returned to the Thanksgiving feast an hour after he had left—with *two* gallons of cider, just in case. He didn't want to make the trip again.

If you live in a rural area, you know the feeling. You get used to scheduling your shopping trips, and keeping lists of what to get next time out. Where does the stress come in? It's the feeling of isolation. If you needed help right away, how long would it take to get there? If you needed to get somewhere right away, how long would you have to travel? We have also observed that marriages can get strained when the partners have few other social outlets, and that creates more stress. Stay-at-home moms with young children can also go stir-crazy without close neighbors, child-care centers, or Ronald McDonald as diversions.

Earlier we noted the modern trend of "cashing out"—quitting a high-stress, city job for some cottage business in the country. People are quitting the rat race for the pace of a rural existence. But it's a tradeoff. The peace and quiet of the country can ease your stress. It's usually a safer atmosphere, too. But if you're used to having everything you need within five minutes, and a lot of entertainment options, it will be quite an adjustment.

What to do?

Much of this is good old common sense, but there's a mental focus involved too.

Plan ahead. Keep a shopping list. Stockpile extra supplies. Be sure to consult everyone in the family before you head out, so you can pick up something they need.

Connect with your neighbors. Obviously, you'll be more reliant on your neighbors, even if they're a mile away. In an emergency, you might need their help, or they yours.

Create contingency plans. What if you have a heart attack? What if the house burns down? What if you have to rush to your dying grandmother's bedside? Anticipate emergencies, so you don't have to worry about them so much.

Delight in simple joys. The slower pace might have you climbing the walls, unless you slow *yourself* down. Enjoy watching a sunset. Learn to meditate. Play cards with your family. And try to be grateful for a hard day's work.

24. How unpleasant are your neighbors or neighborhood?

As a youth, Tom lived for a time in a divided neighborhood. His was one of only a few Protestant families on the block. All the other kids were Catholic, going to parochial schools, and they made fun of Tom. Because he went to a public school, he was known as a "pub," and he was teased for being different.

We hasten to add that the teasing has gone the other way in many Protestant neighborhoods. Catholics, Jews, and atheists, Blacks, Asians, and Latinos have all been made to feel unwelcome. Sometimes the treatment turns violent, but most often it's just unpleasant. People glare at you, ignore your greetings, turn the other way as you pass.

Sometimes it has nothing to do with race or religion—people are just rude. Tom had a next-door neighbor who put up a solid fence between their yards. When Tom painted his own side of it, the neighbor demanded that Tom "finish the job" by painting the other side, too. Of course the same neighbor complained when leaves from Tom's tree fell in his yard.

Neighborhoods can be great places of friendship and support. It's wonderful when people bake cookies for newcomers or bring chicken soup for sick folks. In communities all over the world, you can see neighbors shoveling one another's snow, throwing block parties, or chatting over the back fence. The stress of modern life can be eased by good neighbors—but it can be increased by unpleasant neighbors. You live with these people, so the stress accumulates day by day. It's hard to get away from it.

What to do?

If you're dealing with overt racial or religious terrorism, that's more than this little stress book can tackle. If you're determined to stay and fight for your rights, more power to you—but you've entered a battle, and battles are by nature stressful. If you can't take the stress, there's no shame in moving to a more pleasant place. But if the "unpleasantness" of your community is less severe, here are some ways you might turn it around.

Start a social thing. Throw a party, an ice cream social, a barbecue, something for all your neighbors. Don't wait for them to invite you to an event. Take the reins yourself and plan a bash.

Be a friend. Sometimes we don't notice how unpleasant *we* are. We're waiting for others to reach out to us, but we're sticking to ourselves, ignoring our neighbors in the street, letting our leaves blow onto their lawns. Maybe you don't need to throw a party, just knock on their door and say hi.

Address specific disputes. If there's a specific problem that has alienated a neighbor, talk about it. How can you get on good terms again? Unless your neighbor is totally unreasonable, give in. Take a conciliatory stance; you want peace more than victory.

Build good fences. "Good fences make good neighbors," wrote Robert Frost. Psychologists have tapped that wisdom to develop the whole notion of "boundaries" in your relationships with parents, spouses, and children. Now, finally, we can apply Frost's adage literally—to our neighbors. Disputes arise when it's not clear whose responsibility is whose. When you clarify that (building fences, sometimes literally), you lessen the confusion that can cause stress. But be sure to observe the fifty-five percent rule. Meet your neighbors a little more than halfway. Mow a few strips of their lawn. Rake some of their leaves.

Let it be. Sometimes you can do everything right and your neighbors are still surly. Then, as much as possible, let it go. Stop fretting about it. Try to be a good neighbor, but don't let your bad neighbors get you down. Ask them politely to stop playing "Smoke on the Water" at 3 A.M. If they persist, invest in earplugs. (Calling the authorities will probably cause more trouble than it's worth.) Find your friendships elsewhere—at work, at the gym, at church, in some hobby or group activity. Your home will become a campground, not a community. It's where you sleep, but maybe not where you do a lot of living. That's sad, but it's not worth getting stressed over.

PART SIX

Stress Events

THE phone rings at four o'clock in the morning, waking you up. That sets in motion a series of stress-related events. At first, coming out of a deep sleep, you take a moment to figure out what's happening. You're in bed. It's still dark. Is that a real phone or a dream phone? It's still ringing — must be real.

For most people, late-night phone calls mean trouble. So you begin to worry. What could it be? A loved one lost? An accident? Someone is dying and needs your help? You haven't even touched the phone yet, and your heart is already racing as your mind careens through the possibilities.

You pick up the phone and utter a bleary "Hello?" But your mind is now clicking on all cylinders. Before you hear the voice on the other end, you've narrowed down the options — and you're already planning your response. If it's your parents, you can hop in the car in a few minutes, be there in two hours, call into work at eight o'clock to get someone to cover for you. Wide awake now, you're calling signals like a quarterback.

"Uh, is Hank there?" a teenage voice crackles.

"Hank?" you say. "There's no one named Hank here."

"Uh, sorry. Wrong number, I guess."

False alarm. You can go back to sleep now. Or can you? Your body has just been pumping adrenaline, and you feel like you've just been to Starbucks. You get up and pace. You rearrange your kitchen cabinets. You watch a dumb movie on television. And in an hour you start yawning again. Your body has completed its adrenaline buzz and now you can get back to dreamland. But it will be especially hard to get up when the alarm goes off.

We might call that a mini-stress event. Because it's a false alarm, there's no lasting effect. For that hour or so, however, your system plays out its own war drama. The threat of danger gets you thinking super clearly and your body gets ready to rumble. If it would have been a real emergency, that adrenaline would have helped you shower and dress in record time, drive like Richard Petty, and make whatever quick decisions were necessary. The continuance of the crisis would keep the adrenaline pumping through your body for a while. Eventually you'd crash.

We're wired with a fight-or-flight mechanism, and it's as old as the caveman. When we sense danger, our bodies instinctively gear up for action.

The same is true whenever a car swerves in front of us on the highway. Jolted from our daydreaming, we see everything more clearly. Time seems to slow down for us because our senses are working double time. Arms and legs get a shot of energy as we grip the steering wheel or jam on the brakes. Once the crisis is averted, we gasp for breath. We're tired, maybe even sore, as our bodies recover. Ten minutes later, or maybe an hour, we're back to normal, although the scene might creep into a dream and we might have achy muscles for a day or two.

In these mini-events, we see a pattern:

1. Instinctive response (fight or flight)
2. Recovery
3. Restored equilibrium

Simply put, we gear up for a crisis, we gear down, and then we sail along at an even keel. The gearing up takes a moment, the gearing down takes a while, and we're at equilibrium until the next crisis comes along.

What if those mini-crises turned into major disasters? Say the phone call brought news of the death of a dear relative. Say the swerving car caused an accident, a totaled car, perhaps an injury. What then?

The same pattern occurs, but it's stretched out. Your instinctive response may last for several hours as you make travel plans, administer first aid, or file accident reports. You'll be energized to meet the immediate need. But when the effects of a crisis last longer, your recovery will last longer. If you have suffered a loss of some kind, you will need to proceed through the stages of grieving: denial, anger, bargaining, depression, and acceptance. That may take years.

---

25. Have you experienced a major stress event in the last two years? A major event would be comparable to a death in the immediate family, divorce, job loss, a new marriage, or diagnosis of a major illness.

VARIOUS EVENTS CAN CAUSE MAJOR STRESS IN YOUR LIFE. WE'VE listed the most common. The major stressors fall into three broad categories.

Love—breakup of a primary relationship, or losing a loved one through death or a move.

Life—a jolting of your normal patterns through job change, marriage or divorce, move, injury, illness.

Loss—losing relationship, employment, opportunities, health, abilities, or property.

(Certainly there's overlap among these three categories. The death of a spouse, for instance, would be all three.)

How do you know when a stress event is major? Think in terms of a bomb going off in the middle of your life. Major stress events tend to affect everything else in your life. They may not shut you down entirely—you may still go to work after a divorce, but it will be much harder to focus on your work.

Years ago, an attempt was made to quantify the effect of various life events. Assuming that stress hurts the immune system, researchers studied people's health and the stress events they'd gone through. Then they gave a score to each type of event, according to its ability to affect a person's health. The major stressors, in order, were:

Death in the immediate family
Separation or divorce
Being jailed
Pregnancy, new baby
Loss of job or bankruptcy
Marriage in the immediate family
Major change in financial situation
Injury or major illness in family

Any attempt to place a number on an "explosion" in your life is doomed to fail. You're an individual, and no one can know the precise amount of suffering you feel when you lose a loved one or a job. But we know that major stress events can rock your world, and they'll keep rocking it for a couple of years.

The Stress Test asks about events in the last two years. That doesn't mean that after 24 months you're magically healed of all your pain. But it does reflect the length of time most people take to recover from major stress events.

Tom has worked extensively with divorced people. Time and again, he has heard people say, "I don't know what's wrong with me. It's been six months since my marriage broke up. I should be over it by now." He keeps telling them, "Two years. Give it two years." And that's usually the case. If there are extenuating circumstances, recovery can take up to five years, but two is pretty standard.

The death of a spouse may require less time to recover. Because it's irrevocable, people get through the denial stage fairly quickly, and there's not much bargaining to do. Some religious traditions observe a one-year mourning period, and that corresponds to the normal recovery process, though it may be longer if there are other issues involved.

---

26. Have you experienced one or more moderate stress events in the last month? A moderate stress event would be comparable to a relationship conflict, a parent/child conflict, a significant change in financial or job status, a major project or assignment, or a conflict within your primary social circle.

IF A MAJOR STRESS EVENT IS A BOMB GOING OFF IN YOUR LIFE, A moderate stress event is a pipe bursting. It's a big problem for a short time. You have to clean up one or two compartments in your life, but you don't have to completely rebuild.

For that reason, we ask about moderate events in the last month. These are events that may take a few weeks to deal with. You have a fight with your spouse or child and for a while you're tiptoeing around each other. You get a promotion at work and it takes you six weeks to feel at home with your new responsibilities.

Remember, though, that we're talking about *events*. This is not an ongoing problem with your primary relationship or continuing dissatisfaction with your job. This is a blowup with your boss. It's the two-week project that you're given two days to finish. It's making your spouse sleep on the couch. It's something that happens that disrupts part of your life for a matter of weeks.

Don't underestimate the power of these moderate events. They won't reshape your life like a divorce or job loss, but they may spike your stress levels to dangerous heights. When you're breathing fire at your spouse, it doesn't really matter that you'll be whispering sweet nothings by next Tuesday — right now you are super stressed and it's hurting you.

People often overlook positive stressors. A move to a new community may seem like fun, but it will also stress you. A new project at work may excite you, but it's still stressful, even if you enjoy it. Watching your kid star in the school play is a delight, but you're in a panic until the final bows. That's a moderate stress event — nothing you can't handle by itself, but combined with other events, bad environments, and aggravators, you may have a problem.

Understand, however, that certain events will affect each person differently. We could have offered you a checklist of life events for you to check off, determining your stress score. But that takes your judgment out of the picture. Use your own smarts to determine whether an event has stressed you majorly, moderately, or so little that you can ignore it.

A friend of ours recently relocated with his family to take a new job in a different part of the country. He's regretting it now. They've made no friends in the new area. They hate it there. Our friend is experiencing panic attacks as he worries about the effect of his decision on his family. His wife cries every day, missing her friends back home. There's no question about it. For this family, which had never moved before, this relocation was a major stress event. It may take them up to two years to recover from it and get used to their new home.

But Tom talked with another woman recently who was moving across the country for the second time in five years. Tom anticipated that this might be difficult for her, but she responded, "My dad was in the military. When I was growing up, we moved every two years. It's no big deal." For this woman, a cross-country move was hardly even a moderate stress event.

So gauge the impact of the events of your life. Divorce; the death of a spouse, parent, or child; the loss of a full-time job— these will always be major stressors. But a move, a job change, a death in your extended family, a breakup in a dating relationship (or with a friend)—these could go either way. Is it an explosion or a bursting pipe? It's your call.

27./28. Of the major stressors, have you experienced more than one in the last two years? Of the moderate stressors, have you experienced more than one in the last month?

AS WE'VE SAID, STRESS HAS A NORMAL PATTERN: INSTINCTIVE RESPONSE, recovery, equilibrium. Stuff happens, you get over it, you're back to normal. But what happens when a second stress event occurs before you're fully recovered from the first one? What happens if a third or fourth stress event complicates the picture? Then you could be in trouble.

We've seen this pattern often with divorced people. As they're recovering from the stress of their divorce, they lose concentration at their job. Their work suffers, and sometimes they get fired. That double whammy puts them over the edge.

Or often within a year of the divorce, they'll meet someone new. Because they're very needy, they jump into this new relationship with both feet, even though they still have a lot of recovering to do. They storm ahead, and soon they're very attached emotionally, involved physically, and possibly talking remarriage.

Several things can happen here, and even if they're good, they're bad. The new relationship could break up, and the pain of this second split just adds to the first, creating excessive stress. But let's say the new relationship is a smashing success and they get married. Remarriage is also a significant stressor. Life patterns change. There may be a move involved. If there are children, the stress of creating a blended family or stepfamily is also considerable.

Our point is simple: After the stress of one major event, a second event would be extremely dangerous. There's always the possibility that bad things will just happen to you, but don't take unnecessary chances.

What to do?

In most cases you have little control over stress events. A loved one dies — that's not your decision. If your company gets sold and you get downsized, there's not a lot you can do about it. As hard as people try to divorce-proof their marriages, some spouses still get abandoned. Accidents happen. You catch diseases. To a great extent, stress events are the luck of the draw.

That makes our prescription a bit iffy. You can't inoculate yourself against stress events, but there are a few things you can do to lessen their impact.

Let the healing happen. First of all, accept the normal processes. Don't get anxious about the stress you feel over a death, divorce, or major life change. You're *supposed* to feel bad at first, and then you'll feel better and better over the next two years or so.

Don't get stuck in denial. The first stage of grief is denial. You want to think the bad event never happened. That's natural and even healthy — for a while. But if you're still questioning the reality of the situation three or four months after the event, then your healing is being delayed.

Protect yourself. If you break your arm, the doctors put it in a cast, immobilizing it for a healing period and protecting it so it doesn't get broken again. If your heart gets broken, through death or a breakup or some other crisis, you need to protect it so it doesn't get smashed again. That's why we urge people to avoid romantic relationships for two years after a divorce or the death of a spouse. And don't make any life-changing decisions until you're ready. In the emotion of the moment, people can decide things that just cause more stress. Be careful about that.

Find supporters. You need good friends during your recovery, and a lot of them. Some people, especially men, try to close up when they suffer pain. They prefer to deal with it alone. Take your "cave time" if you need it, but don't sever your connections with others. Having a handful of affirming friends will aid your recovery.

Get counsel from those who have been there. As Tom runs divorce-recovery seminars, he regularly hears that the most valuable aspect is merely the connection with other people who have suffered the same thing. "I felt all alone," people say, "and now I know others feel this way too." The sharing of grief is a healing activity.

Look for a pattern. You don't want to blame yourself for everything that happens to you, but if you seem especially "accident prone" lately, you may want to evaluate your behavior. Are you doing things that lead to broken relationships, job terminations, or traffic accidents? A counselor or close friend may help you get perspective.

Use the Stress Quotient. When you understand the different sources of stress, you can use one to counter the others. That is, if stress events (which you can't control) are raising your stress levels into the danger zone, then compensate by easing up on your stress environments or aggravators or by improving your stress fitness (all of which you *can* control). That's what this book is all about—taking control of the different aspects of your stress.

PART SEVEN

Stress Aggravators

EVERY so often you'll get a mailing from some charity urging you to give because they have a "matching grant." That is, some rich person or company has promised to give the same amount the charity raises through private donations. Your gift is effectively doubled. If you give ten dollars, the benefactor gives ten, and so the charity gets twenty. Sometimes a charity can line up two or three matching grants, so your gift is tripled or even quadrupled. But you have to give something to make it happen. The matching grants kick in only when you make your donation.

Stress aggravators are something like that, only in a negative sense. If you have no stress (or little stress), you don't have to worry about the aggravators. But when stress starts to bother you, those aggravators are right there to double or triple its effect. Some of the aggravators are attitudes that amplify problems or keep you from resolving them. These attitudes are sparked by stress and intensify your stressful feelings. Other aggravators are patterns of behavior that tend to make your stressful situations worse. But with all of them, because they multiply your stress, as you work at reducing their effect, your Stress Quotient will decrease substantially.

---

29. Do you tend to make "mountains out of molehills," taking a stressful event and magnifying it, or obsessing about the event?

"PAY NO ATTENTION TO THE MAN BEHIND THE CURTAIN." IN *The Wizard of Oz*, Dorothy realizes that the wizard is not the huge, fearsome image in front of her, but a funny little man at the controls behind the curtain. As long as she was facing the giant image, she was paralyzed by fear. She was stressed. But once little Toto cut the wizard down to size, Dorothy could get down to business.

We often do the same thing in stressful situations. Our fears inflate our obstacles into huge images that scare us even more. Maybe you're afraid of public speaking, and you're asked to say a few words to your department next Monday about the project you're working on. All weekend you obsess about it. You'll be talking to ten people, but you start to imagine fifty. They're your friends, but you expect them to be grading you on your presentation. You've been asked to say "a few words," but you're thinking of it as a speech and worrying that you won't have enough to say. The night before you're tossing and turning, and then you're afraid you'll fail for lack of sleep. When the alarm goes off, you feel lousy, so you call in sick.

Let's tack a fun conclusion onto this story. In the middle of the day, your office mate calls you at home, saying, "We're going to have this meeting without you, so fill me in on this project of yours."

You know this stuff inside and out, so you breeze through the main points and say, "There. That should give you enough to report to the department."

"I don't have to," he replies. "You just did. I had you on the speakerphone." And you hear the department burst into applause.

That wasn't so bad now, was it? It wasn't lack of knowledge causing the stress, or a lack of communication skill. It was an irrational fear that compounded the stress of talking to a group.

What to do?

Feelings of anxiety are very real. They may be based on unrealistic fears, but the feelings can cause genuine problems. In our story, the illness that caused you to call in sick wasn't faked. People are essentially paralyzed by their anxious thoughts. So you can't just say, "Get over it." But you can start to pull the curtain aside to reveal the tiny problems that are masquerading as big ones. By *seeing* the situation differently, you can begin *feeling* differently about it.

Imagine the worst-case scenario. This seems like you're playing into your anxiety, but it will actually help. Face your fears by imagining that everything bad happens just as you're afraid it will. You speak in front of the group and you're tongue-tied and they all laugh at you. That will certainly make you feel bad, but you'll survive. In most cases, even imagining the worst that could happen, you'd still get through it—even though there might be pain or embarrassment involved.

Choose to live by probabilities, not possibilities. Ninety percent of the things we worry about never happen. So why waste nine-tenths of your life for nothing? And does worrying really help you deal with the other ten percent? Probably not. When you obsess about the bad things that *could* happen to you, a bad thing is *already* happening to you: your obsession. Don't trade your valuable peace of mind for an obsession about something that probably won't happen anyway!

Get right with God. People who have a strong relationship with God tend to keep their problems in perspective. Instead of amplifying the things that could go wrong, they trust that God will work things out for good. That doesn't mean God zaps away all your difficulties, but there's a sense that everything is going according to plan, that God is in control. This assurance yields a kind of inner peace that makes molehills out of mountains.

See people in their underwear. We're not talking about the Victoria's Secret catalog. This is an age-old way to get over the jitters of encountering other people. If you're uneasy with public speaking, or in a job interview, or just nervous about not making the grade with the folks you're meeting with, well, just imagine them in their underwear. That strips away pretensions of rank or position and reveals that they're just people too, like you. (If underwear is a bit intimate for you, imagine playing volleyball with them, or having a backyard barbecue. Or think of them in their "grubbies" cleaning the garage or working on the car.)

Accept setbacks as adventures. Part of the mountain-out-of-a-molehill attitude is "I'm jinxed! Nothing good ever happens to me!" Tame that thought by seeing your troubles as challenges. Accept the adventure of overcoming them. Odysseus encountered a pack of troubles on his trip home from the war, and Homer wrote an adventure book about him (*The Odyssey*). Write your own adventure book, beginning with the difficulties you're facing today.

Consider taking medication for your obsessive-compulsive tendencies. There's no miracle drug that will solve all your stress problems, but in certain cases medication helps. If your stress recovery is hampered by your obsessions over every little thing, the right drug might help you get back on track. See a doctor, counselor, or psychiatrist.

30. Do you tend to be your own worst enemy by taking an event and beating yourself up over it, blaming yourself or berating yourself over that event?

OUR FRIEND TED IS SCRUPULOUS TO A FAULT. IF HE FINDS A TEN dollar bill on the sidewalk, he wonders whether he should report it on his income tax. Well, maybe that's an exaggeration, but recently he told us about renting a car and having some minor problem with it. While driving on the highway, the car sputtered and stalled a couple of times, disabling the power steering and brakes. Ted pulled over, fiddled with the carburetor, and drove on. When he returned the car, he was asked, "Everything all right with it?" and he nodded.

But later he remembered the problem with the engine and felt guilty about not reporting it. Maybe someone else would rent that car and have the same problem, but he'd get into an accident, he fretted. Maybe there'd be innocent blood on his hands!

"I'm a liar," he told us. "I said everything was fine when it wasn't. I'm as bad as a politician!"

No, not that bad, we assured him. The truth is, it's great to be honest, but Ted's being unreasonable. It makes no sense for him to beat himself up over a silly thing like that.

When people like Ted beat themselves up over minor problems, they have a problem of perception. Several factors could be viewed improperly. They might have a false view of the situation; such people blame themselves for everything, even when it's not their fault. Sometimes it's an enlarged view of minor faults; we all goof from time to time, but these people magnify their minor mistakes to Jurassic proportions. Or they have a distorted view of themselves; because they magnify all their flaws, they see themselves as bad, worthless, morally bankrupt people. And sometimes they have an exalted view of their own influence; this is ironic, because such people tend to be self-effacing, and yet they're convinced that their actions are going to bring ruin to everyone else in the whole world.

What to do?

When people are their own worst enemies, they're not seeing how things really are, but distorting the truth in order to blame themselves.

See the gray. Part of the problem is black-and-white thinking. Something bad happens and you're sure it's either all your fault or not your fault at all. In black-and-white thinking, you're either a perfect person or the scum of the earth. But the truth lies somewhere between those extremes. Maybe you were wrong, but so were others. You're certainly not perfect, but you're not a mass murderer either. Open your eyes to the shades of gray between the black and the white. Accept yourself as a flawed but well-meaning person, and learn to share blame when appropriate.

Give yourself a good talking to. Counselors often refer to self-talk, the conversations you have with yourself. When people are their own worst enemies, they often insult themselves. "You loser! Can't you do anything right?" You've got to turn that around. Change your self-talk from bad to good, from tearing down to building up. You may *feel* guilty or ashamed in a certain situation, but use your mind to understand the truth and fight your feelings with facts. "Sure, I could have done better, but I did pretty well." Careful—don't overdo the compliments. A good "gray" analysis—with self-affirmation but room for improvement—can help you see things more clearly.

Be your own imaginary friend. Think about how your best friend behaves toward you. Does he or she yell at you whenever you do something wrong? Does the person point out all your flaws? Does this friend predict that you'll never succeed at anything you try? Probably not. Good friends support us, encourage us, compliment us, give us hope. Sure, they give us a swift kick when we need it, but they don't kick us when we're down. They pick us back up. Why can't you do that for yourself? You had an imaginary friend when you were four, sipping tea with you in the sandbox—why not now? Get that imaginary friend to say all the good things you need to hear.

31. Do you put things off until the last minute— procrastinating to the point of making projects worse than they need to be?

AS WE WRITE THIS PARAGRAPH, THIS BOOK WAS SUPPOSED TO BE finished six weeks ago. But we procrastinated. We had the contract, had the deadline, had the research done. We just needed to write it. But we put it off.

The last few weeks have been murderous. Because of our earlier procrastination, we really had to get busy. We canceled other appointments, postponed other projects, and watched the dishes pile up in the sink as we struggled to meet the extension of the extension of the extended deadline. We'd like to say this is a rare occurrence, but it's not. For both of us, procrastination is a major stress aggravator.

We could tell you all sorts of stories about the effect of procrastination in our lives, but not now. Maybe later.

The point is: As we struggled to finish writing this, we were far more stressed than we needed to be—all because we put off the project for too long. There was a bit of stress at the beginning of the project: "How are we going to do this?" And that stress fed into our procrastination, which of course made the stress worse.

If you're also a procrastinator, you know the feeling. You like to say that deadlines bring out the best work in you, but in fact you never start working on something until right before it's due. Then you have a sudden high-stress period of work, which may set you back on other projects, which you'll have to catch up on later. You're always chasing some deadline, and you never feel that you're ahead of the game.

What to do?

Of course it often comes down to good, old-fashioned discipline, but here are a few tricks that might make it easier.

Break it down. Some jobs can be daunting because they're

just too big. So don't think in terms of writing a book. Write a chapter or a page. Don't paint the house, paint a room, paint a wall, or buy the paint. Or choose a color. Get some small piece of the project you can start on and complete in a short time. Then take the next piece. Writer Anne Lamott tells of her ten-year-old brother agonizing over a report about birds he had to write for school. "He was at the kitchen table close to tears . . . immobilized by the hugeness of the task ahead. Then my father sat down beside him . . . and said, 'Bird by bird, buddy. Just take it bird by bird.'" And that became the name of her fine book on how to write: *Bird by Bird*.[15]

Choose your distractions. To work well, some people need music playing or neighbors arguing or trains chugging by across the street. Some people think they need distractions when those things really just distract them. If you commit yourself to working on a project, it's like a marriage—you have to forsake all others. Take the phone off the hook. Forget this multi-tasking trend. Focus on that one thing until you've done today's piece of it.

Give yourself rewards and penalties. If you meet your goals for the morning, good for you! Take a break. But don't let your break last all afternoon. Sometimes missed deadlines will carry their own penalties, but try to find your own deterrents. If you've broken down the project to a series of partial deadlines, then penalize yourself for each one of those you miss. In the fall, Tom has a great reward/penalty for his weekend work. If he doesn't get it done Saturday, he has to do it Sunday afternoon—and he doesn't get to watch football on TV.

Find people to hold you accountable. Most people won't nag you unless you give them permission. So find the people you need to spur you along, and give them explicit permission to ask you about your upcoming projects. (Be careful about asking your spouse to do this. Nagging can torpedo a marriage, whether you ask for it or not.)

32. Do you tend to take on too much responsibility, saying "yes" to too many things, only to find yourself feeling overwhelmed?

WE LOVE THE COMMERCIAL WHERE A HARRIED WORKER IS ANSWER-
ing the phone, saying, "I can do that," "I can do that," "I can do
that." Then he hangs up and moans, "How am I going to do that?"

Many people get overwhelmed because they just can't say
no. When they're asked to do things, they cheerfully agree, even
though they really don't have the time. People-pleasing is the
underlying issue here. These yes-sayers want to be liked, and
they're afraid to disappoint others. Sometimes they're driven by
a passion for accomplishment. They want to do it all, so they
fill their plate to overflowing.

Reality crashes down upon these people. Ultimately, they wonder "How am I going to do that?" Others learn that you can't always
count on the people-pleasers. Oh, they'll promise you the moon,
but they won't always come through.

You can get away with saying yes if people aren't asking you
to do a lot. But when there are great needs at your job, in your
home, in your community, in your church or your volunteer activity, then there are many requests. Because of your inability to say
no, you take the stress of the situation on yourself. Obligations pile
up, and stress is compounded. You end up missing deadlines, doing
shoddy work, or bailing out at the last minute. Ironically, this behavior makes enemies rather than friends, so your desire for
people-pleasing ultimately backfires.

What to do?

There's nothing wrong with wanting people to like you. But it
becomes problematic when you try to earn people's favor by taking on too much. Wise scheduling habits will help, but you also
need to develop a sturdier sense of yourself.

Believe in boundaries. When Tom is invited to speak at seminars, the people-pleaser in him wants to help out, but he could be gone every weekend. In fact, he did that for a while—until his wife protested. He had to set limits on his speaking engagements, for the good of his marriage, his children, and his own well-being. Recently, Tom was asked to give a talk on "Caring for the Caregiver." He was instinctively saying yes until he realized this would be his only Saturday at home in a month. As a caregiver, he had to care for himself and say no. The first step toward tackling a people-pleasing problem is to understand that boundary setting is a good thing, not a selfish thing. Your own health and family concerns are more important than the other needs that come your way.

Take time to think about it. People can be pushy. Don't let them drag an instant commitment out of you if you need to mull it over a bit. If they can't wait a day for your answer, let them find someone else.

Are you the best person for the job? Sometimes people ask you because they don't have enough imagination. No offense, but there might be seven other people around who could do the job better than you could. Learn who these people are and start giving out their phone numbers. Everyone will thank you, and this frees you up to do the things you're best at.

Schedule rest periods. If you're flying in from Phoenix at 3:00, don't schedule a meeting for 3:15. Even if your flight is on time, you'll need to catch your breath. Don't stack your activities too tightly.

Remember Murphy's Law. If anything can go wrong, it will. Put some Murphy's padding in your schedule. Maybe under optimum conditions you can do this job by 4:00, but optimum conditions are a fantasy. Something will go haywire. Don't promise it until 5:00.

Load in some jobs you can toss. If you've scheduled this project for George and that one for Mary, and you've promised to take your kids bowling, and you can't bear to disappoint any of them, don't take on additional jobs for Wendell, Sue, and Julio. Put some optional things in your schedule—writing your novel or filing your old reports or anything that doesn't have to get done immediately. Then if other jobs overwhelm you, you can toss those extra projects and no one cares.

33. Do you have compulsive or addictive behaviors such as smoking, overeating, drinking, gambling, or overspending?

RICHARD RUNS A BUSINESS OUT OF HIS HOME, AND LATELY HE'S been getting a lot of work. That's great, but also stressful. Yet Richard has now discovered a way to escape from the stress. He plays computer games.

Whenever he feels overwhelmed by the amount of work he has to do, he decides to fire up a game and play for a half-hour. He assumes that will clear his mind, relax him, and help him start fresh on his next project. Not so. It takes over his mind. As he maneuvers to shoot down aliens, he is hardly relaxing. And the half-hour quickly becomes an hour, even two. Before he realizes it, the afternoon is half gone and he still has a pile of work to do. Richard thinks the game will alleviate his stress, but it actually aggravates it.

Computer game playing is a rather recent entry into a set of compulsive-addictive behaviors that are sparked by stress and only serve to make stress worse. Some turn to junk food, then feel sluggish, fat, and down on themselves. Some smoke to relax, but become nervous instead. Some gamble to escape, but just watch their money escape from their wallets. Some "have a few drinks" to unwind from all their stress, then black out for the evening and wake up so hung over that they lose another day. And when the going gets tough, some go shopping, resulting in huge credit card balances they're now less able to pay.

People turn to these behaviors in times of stress, hoping their problems will be solved. While some of these activities are fine in moderation, stress makes a person tend to overdo it. That's when the behavior becomes compulsive, addictive, and dangerous.

The actions can start as an outlet for nervous energy. Richard's tired of crunching numbers and wants to crunch some spaceships—no problem. But soon it becomes an escape. As long as he's playing, he can forget about his stressful life, and isn't that sweet? Gambling casinos are designed as alternate worlds, where we can live our fantasies and leave the real world behind.

And how many people "drink to forget," seeking a buzz that will mask their worries?

Behavioral addictions—gambling, sex, relationships, working, shopping, eating, and drinking—establish a new mental equilibrium. When people feel overstressed, they feel out of balance, and so they try to restore that sense of equilibrium through the compulsive-addictive behaviors.

What to do?

In serious cases of addiction or compulsion, see a counselor. We also recommend the various "Anonymous" groups that have sprung up for different addictions. This book cannot begin to address all the issues involved in addiction. But in less serious cases, a few strategies may help you deal with your stress without these aggravators.

See the reality. Understand the toll this behavior takes on you. See how it aggravates your stress. Reveal its broken promises. Count up the time and money you've wasted on it. How much less stressful would your life be if you had all of that back?

Put limits on your unwinding. Be vigilant about your down time. If you want to take a break and play computer games, set a timer for a half-hour and stop then. If you want to take a shopping trip, put a limit on the time and money you'll spend. Have a cookie or two to celebrate the work you've done, but don't spend the day munching the whole bag. Define what moderation is for you, and stick with it.

Find substitutes. One strategy to fight addictions is to replace the behavior with something similar, but not as dangerous. A computer-game addict might take that break to answer e-mail— it's on the computer, it's fun, it's less compulsive. A gambler might join a just-for-fun football pool with friends. Be careful, though, that the substitute won't lead you into a new addiction (for example, people recovering from addiction to alcohol or drugs often take up smoking).

Cut your supply. The person trying to quit smoking has to throw out all ashtrays, matches, lighters, and of course, cigarettes.

Richard may want to delete the game files from his computer. The shopaholic should probably cut up a few credit cards. Get rid of your paraphernalia, and it will be harder to resume the behavior.

Find accountability. This is a major factor of the Alcoholics Anonymous program. Members hold each other accountable for their commitment to quit. If you're troubled by a compulsive-addictive behavior, get people to check up on you. Give them permission to ask you how you're doing. And never, ever, lie to them.

34. Do you have a hard time forgiving others, holding on to grievances or your anger for longer than you should?

TOM HAS COUNSELED HUNDREDS, MAYBE THOUSANDS, OF DIVORCED people. Talk about stress! Not only does divorce shake up a person's life, it often implants deep anger and resentment. The major issue at Tom's divorce recovery seminars is forgiveness. Some people take the challenge and let go of their hurt feelings. Others cling to their pain, the last vestige of the life they once had. As Tom likes to say, "You either get better or bitter."

Anger is supposed to fade. Time is supposed to heal your wounds. But when you cling to your hurts, they take residence within you. It's as if you *become* your pain. If you weren't angry, you don't know who you'd be.

Relational stress is compounded when people harbor ill feelings. The events that caused the initial problem are relived, reviewed from every angle, zoomed in on, amplified, and studied in detail. Shakespeare wrote that cowards die a thousand deaths; well, bitter people suffer a thousand hurts as they keep going over the one that initially wounded them.

If the other person is far away now, you nurse your wounds privately. But if you still see the backstabber on a regular basis, those wounds are reopened each time. And sometimes you take out your bitterness on others. You'll never fall in love again. You'll never trust another friend. You snap at your children or coworkers even though you realize it's not about them, it's about the pain you carry inside.

It's time to do something about that.

What to do?

The basic prescription is simple: Let go. That's all forgiveness is, a letting go of your bad feelings. It's easy to say, hard to do, but absolutely necessary.

Seek understanding if possible. One maddening thing about broken relationships is that you're left with so many things to say. You just want the other person to understand how he or she has hurt you. This isn't always possible, but sometimes you can write a letter or have a meeting and communicate what's necessary. In either form, be sure to communicate information — don't let your feelings take over. If you meet, be sure to protect yourself by meeting in a public place, with your own transportation. And don't be disappointed if the other person still just doesn't get it. But it's worth a try.

Crash the symbols. We have found that symbolic acts can help people let go of their bitterness. Write down the offense and burn the paper as you "give up" your anger. Stand in the rain for an hour to let the pain wash away. Visit a children's hospital as a commitment to your own healing. Bury a stuffed animal as your way of saying that your pain has died. Get a tattoo that says "Free," and touch it whenever you begin to dredge up the old wounds. In some symbolic way, commit yourself to letting go.

See forgiveness as a selfish act. At this point, forgiveness has little to do with the other person. Most non-forgivers have the attitude, "I won't let you get away with this!" But you shouldn't forgive others for *their* benefit; it's for *you*. It's an act of self-preservation. Bitterness is ruining *your* life; it's not hurting the other person at all. When you spend your life keeping score, you end up the loser. Remember the ad that said, "Living well is the best revenge"? Forget it. *Forgiveness* is the best revenge.

Accept your own need for forgiveness. All of us have done things for which we need forgivness — by our parents, by our children, by our God. When you harbor bitterness, you close yourself off from *receiving* forgiveness. Once you see yourself as a fallible person in need of a break, you'll be more apt to forgive others.

PART EIGHT

Stress Fitness

SOME people just seem to handle stress better than others.

Your whole company may be on the verge of bankruptcy and everyone's losing sleep over it. They're all snapping at each other and making frantic decisions. Except for one guy who stays calm through it all. What's his deal?

Two young mothers visit their children's preschool and learn that their kids, left unsupervised, got into a fight and hurt each other. One mother goes ballistic. The other keeps her cool and handles the situation effectively, attending to the children and confronting the staff. What's the difference between them?

The Stress Test isolates different factors that add up to your Stress Quotient. The struggling company is certainly a high-stress work environment, and the whole staff shares that high stress — including the guy who's not stressed! The preschool episode is certainly a stress event of at least moderate proportions, but both women share the event and only one shows stress.

The difference may be the whole area of stress fitness. Certain life habits can prepare you well for stress. They give you a kind of cushion for the hard knocks of life. Just as aggravators multiply your stress, stress fitness divides it. You still feel the effects of your company's turmoil or your children's pain, but you're not thrown as much. You deal with it better. Some of these habits help your body deal with the physical effects of stress. Others help your mind or spirit find acceptance or resolution more easily.

145

---

35. Do you follow an exercise program each week?

EXERCISE IS ONE OF THE MOST POSITIVE WAYS TO RELEASE STRESS. Many people take medications that send chemicals to the brain, giving a sense of well-being and satisfaction. But research has shown that exercise does basically the same thing, providing endorphins and serotonin to the brain, giving you feelings of well-being and comfort.

When you follow an exercise program, you also undo some of the damage that stress does to your system. Stress can raise your blood pressure and tax your heart. Exercise lowers blood pressure and strengthens your cardiovascular system. Stress tightens you physically; exercise loosens you. If you have muscle spasms or nervous tics or jaw pain stemming from stress, exercise can relax you physically and ease those problems.

What to do?

Find an activity you enjoy. If you hate exercising, you won't do it. Or it will just be stressful for you. Find a way to make it fun.

See your doctor. It's always best to consult your physician before starting an exercise program.

Commit to it. You can ease into it, but ultimately try to schedule exercise at least three times a week, for at least half an hour. Once a week is better than no exercise at all, but the three-a-week workouts are most profitable. And even if you're not doing a full workout, do some sort of exercise daily.

Plan for year-round activity. If winter weather makes it difficult to go jogging, have a plan B ready. Join a gym or the local Y or get some home equipment for bad weather days.

Don't get too stressed about it. If you miss a day, don't fret. Just pick up your exercise program the next day. If you feel guilty about not exercising, stop feeling guilty and *do it!* Something is better than nothing. Recent research has verified what many have suspected for a while: the small bits of exercise we do during the day add up. So even if you can't (or won't) start a formal exercise program, take the stairs more often, take walks, carry your kids around. You'll feel the difference.

---

36. Are you good about eating nutritionally balanced and healthy meals? Do you also avoid smoking, excessive alcohol, or caffeine?

GARBAGE IN, GARBAGE OUT. THIS COMPUTER AXIOM APPLIES TO nutrition as well. If you put good stuff into your body, your body will put out a good effort for you. But if you cram your body with junk food, nicotine, alcohol, and caffeine, your body will rebel.

You don't need us to tell you how to eat right. There are plenty of other books on the market that will guide you to good nutrition. But let us steer you toward a balanced, healthy diet. Don't follow the latest fad. Eat a variety of good foods in reasonable proportions. This will give your body the fuel it needs to withstand stressful situations.

Stress actually reduces the amount of vitamins you absorb from food, so you need to eat more to get the same effect. A steady supply of vitamin-rich foods will strengthen your immune system as well, which can be damaged by stress. Unfortunately, when we're stressed and need the most nutrition, we often grab snacks on the run and ignore our need for a healthy diet.

What to do?

Forget the stressful hype. We know people who won't eat fruits or vegetables because of the pesticides used on them. But surely the benefit of the vitamins in these foods outweighs the danger from the traces of chemicals you ingest. Every week, the tabloids crow about some new food benefit or danger. You can get very stressed worrying whether you're eating right. Relax. Stick to your balanced diet and you'll be fine.

Enjoy food, in moderation. The problem with the hype is that we start to fear our food. We sit down to dinner and worry about the carbs in the bread, the fat in the butter, the pesticide in the salad, the preservatives in the salad dressing, the salmonella in the chicken, and the cholesterol in the cordon bleu. Food is a gift to enjoy. Delight in it. But enjoy reasonable portions of your most delightful foods.

When changing your diet, see your doctor. Occasionally, you may need to go on a special diet, but be sure you're under a doctor's supervision.

Consider the family effect. If you're eating with your family, your choice of food will be connected to theirs. That may make it difficult if you're on a special diet and they're not. Food can cause more tension in a family than we expect. You have to eat Grandma's pie so you don't hurt her feelings, even though you're on a low-calorie diet. You're trying to cut out fats, but your spouse insists on meat with gravy. If you can steer through that kind of stress, you're brilliant. Just remember: It's only food.

Practice discipline with chemical substances. We're talking about nicotine, alcohol, and caffeine. All of these have an effect on your body and your stress level. Smoking is just plain bad for you, though trying to quit may be more stressful. Pick the right time and get help. A moderate amount of alcohol or caffeine won't hurt you, unless you have certain health problems, but it's easy to go overboard with either of them. Be smart about them. One's a downer, the other's an upper, and people often use them to manage their stress levels throughout the day. That could be a dangerous pattern to get into. If you "need" that morning coffee and that late-night drink, you're coming close to addiction. Practice discipline with all these substances.

---

37. Do you take regular breaks during the day in order to relax, especially during lunch? Do you also take a regular day off in order to relax or spend time with family and friends?

WE FIND A BRILLIANT IDEA TUCKED AWAY IN THE TEN COMMANDMENTS: "Six days you shall labor and do all your work, but the seventh day is a Sabbath to the LORD your God. On it you shall not do any work . . . For in six days the LORD made the heavens and the earth, the sea, and all that is in them, but he rested on the seventh day. Therefore the LORD blessed the Sabbath day and made it holy" (Exodus 20:9-11).

Even God took a day off! The principle is a healthy one, and much needed in today's nonstop society. We need to take time off in order to be more productive over the long haul.

That also applies to *minutes* off. A full day of work will wear you out if you don't take a few quality breaks along the way. Many companies build these into their daily schedules. If so, you need to take full advantage of them. If you're on your own, you should be sure to take regular breathers.

"Breather" —a great word for it. As you're pushing yourself to work hard, you're stressing your system. Your heart pumps furiously to supply all your blood needs. Your muscles tense. Your brain clicks away. And your breathing grows more rapid. When you take a breather, you get to breathe deeply, to relax your muscles, to get your heart rate down for a while. It's like pushing the reset button on your computer—everything goes back to its original state.

You can derive some benefit by taking a few deep breaths every half-hour or so, but you really need a few substantial breaks during the day—ten to thirty minutes—to relax your system more fully. And you still need a whole day off now and then.

What to do?

Don't cheat yourself out of a break. When you take a break, really relax. Don't talk business. Watch out for business lunches too. They're disguised as breaks, but they're really work. If you do business over lunch, take a walk afterward to clear your head.

Get away. If you can get out of your workplace every so often for a break, that will help. You need a change of scenery and fresh air. Try to get out for lunch. When you eat at work, even in a company cafeteria, you can always be interrupted for business matters. You need at least a brief time away from all that. The same is true in a larger sense for your days off. Get out of town from time to time.

Remember solitude. People need "hang time" with friends, but they also need time alone. "Most people I talk to feel they suffer from not having time to be by themselves," says clinical psychologist Jeffrey Rossman, who runs a health resort in Lenox, Massachusetts.[16] It's harder than ever to withdraw, with beepers and cell phones tracking us down every minute. One woman explained that she felt "like a human *doing* instead of a human *being*," until she started stepping into a closet for forty minutes of solitude each day.[17] You might find a roomier location, and even twenty minutes a day would be helpful, but don't neglect the renewal that comes from solitude.

38. Have you resolved issues or hurts from the past? Are you looking forward to a promising future?

PEOPLE WHO HAVE A POSITIVE OUTLOOK ON LIFE LIVE LONGER. There's a bit of self-fulfilling prophecy at work here. When people, pained by the past, expect only more pain in the future, that's what they find. Others, having recovered from past hurts, expect a brighter future and get it.

It's something like Velcro. This revolutionary fastener is actually a collection of tiny hooks and eyes. The little hooks of one Velcro strip grab onto the little eyes of the other and the two stick together. When people nurse their hurts from the past, they wrap themselves in a kind of emotional Velcro. Then, when new issues come along, they hook onto the old issues and stick there.

Imagine two sisters, Amy and Beth, both told repeatedly by their parents they'd never amount to much. In adulthood, Amy seeks counseling and works through the old issues. She learns that her parents were wrong, that she can accomplish a great deal. She surrounds herself with affirming friends and now holds a good job. Beth, on the other hand, still suffers from very low self-esteem, based on her parents' discouragement. She has never resolved that old issue.

Now, both Amy and Beth are called into their bosses' offices and are told their work isn't up to snuff. If they don't improve, they might be fired.

Amy answers this stress with renewed determination. She resolves to work harder to keep her job. But Beth is destroyed. This new stress sticks to all her old issues. She hears her parents saying, "We told you! You're just no good! You can't do it!" And she concludes that they were probably right all along. While Amy meets her boss's challenge and keeps her job, Beth falls apart and loses hers. Amy's brighter outlook for the future has come true, but Beth's past has pulled her back.

It's amazing how often the past and future collide. Often, similar scenes are played out throughout our lives. If we don't learn from our personal history, we're doomed to repeat it. But if we resolve our past issues, we can move forward to a more positive future. We learn valuable resolution skills we can apply to new issues. If you've conquered your past, the skills will continue to help you through the challenges of the future.

What to do?

Seek counseling. Many issues of the past are so deeply rooted in your life that you need professional help to break free of them.

Review the facts with your family. If your parents were ogres, it might be best *not* to confront them. But many personal issues arise from simple mistakes, misunderstandings, or family crises. If you sit down and talk about the issues with your family, you might reach new understandings that can pave the way to greater emotional health.

Rewrite your personal script. You've been handed a script for the drama of your life. It tells you who you are, what you can and cannot do, perhaps even what you're supposed to say. Who wrote this script? All the forces of your past—parents, teachers, siblings, playmates, old boyfriends or girlfriends. If you let them, they'll script your future, too. Eventually, you should grab this script and rewrite it for yourself. Decide who you are and where you're headed.

Give yourself a support statement. It might help to come up with a statement you can tell yourself when you start hearing the voices of the past pulling you back. Something to silence those voices. "I can do it." Or, "I know God has great plans for me." Or, "How can I look back when the future looks so bright?"

39. Do you have a strong faith, turning your worries over to God? Do you meditate or pray about things that are beyond your control?

MANY TIMES WE'VE NOTED THAT CONTROL IS A MAJOR ISSUE IN stress. Like rats in a cage, we feel more stress when we're not in control. Often we can reduce stress by taking control of a situation, at least in our own minds. But there will always be certain factors beyond our control.

Your college-age daughter starts dating a biker named Spike who has steel bolts through his cheeks. You don't like it, but that's the whole point. You're not supposed to like it.

A tornado starts twisting through your town, randomly leveling homes. You can hide in your basement, but can you do anything to protect your house and belongings?

Your spouse gets very sick and you get the best medical treatment you can afford, but even the doctors aren't sure what to do.

What can you do in situations like that? Well, you can pray.

Many people pray in emergency situations, whether they're religious or not. When they reach the end of themselves, they reach out to the only One who can help. Usually they pray for a particular outcome: *Heal the one I love, spare my home from the twister, introduce my daughter to a nice pre-med student.* These prayers are not always answered the way we want. Tornadoes have devoured the homes of many praying people. Terminal patients have prayed all the way to their graves.

But prayer gives you something else besides a desired outcome. It gives you power, peace, and perspective. You get power to meet the challenges—to rebuild your house, to prepare your family for the death of your spouse, even to make friends with Spike. As C. S. Lewis explains to a skeptical friend in the movie *Shadowlands*, even when prayer doesn't change the circumstances, it changes *us.*

You get a certain peace in the midst of trying times. By praying, you have taken control, and you've given it to someone who knows what to do. You can trust that God will bring you through the situation, whether or not the outcome is the one you want.

And by communicating with God, we inevitably gain a different perspective. We grieve the death of our beloved, but our vision is enlarged to see a greater life beyond. We wonder why our home is blown away, but we realize how trivial our material possessions are. We even learn that Spike is a human being too, no matter how much metal is piercing his body.

What to do?

Set aside a regular time for prayer or meditation. Jesus talked about going into your closet to pray, and that's not a bad idea. Get away from it all and spend some quiet time.

Request, but also rest. Ask God for the things you want, but then take some time to simply rest. Listen. Meditate. You're not dealing with a God.com consumer Web site. You're communing with the Creator of the universe. So take some time to *be*. In some religious traditions, people take a vow of silence from time to time. As the leader of a retreat center explained to Tom once, "Many of us talk to God constantly and wonder why we never hear him answer our prayers. We believe it's largely because we're not taking time to listen."

Breathe your prayers. As you go through the day, take your prayers with you. You don't need to kneel or close your eyes; just take a breath and say, "God, be with me," or something like that.

Pray with others. You can build great relationships by joining others in brief times of prayer. Find groups at your church or synagogue, but also consider starting a group at your workplace, school, or neighborhood. You'll be amazed at how many people are interested. Don't preach or try to convert people—just share your concerns and pray with (and for) one another.

40. Have you set short- and long-term goals, updating them at appropriate intervals?

A FIRST-TIME PLAY DIRECTOR PANICS WHEN THE CAST READS THE script for the first time. They're not very good. If they perform the show like that, the audience will walk out before intermission. But that's why there are rehearsals!

A more experienced director doesn't demand perfection right away. He or she understands there will be steady progress along the way. If you're at the dress rehearsal and the cast is still stumbling over the words, then you can panic. But give it time to grow.

That's what short- and long-term goals give you: a timetable for progress. Some people get so goal-oriented that they increase their stress. You've probably known people like that—Type A whip crackers who have an agenda for every minute of the day. But goals are made for people, not people for goals. Goals should help you know where you're headed in life and how to get there. It's stressful to have no sense of direction and no sense of progress. That's what goals can give you—a few coordinates on the radar screen of life.

What to do?

Develop a personal mission statement. Businesses spend years crafting the perfect statement of who they are and what they're doing. Why can't you? Consider the talents, interests, and responsibilities you have and what you want to do with them. Then write out a statement.

Follow calendar cues. You may already make New Year's resolutions. You probably forget them all by Super Bowl Sunday. Try to take them more seriously. Or maybe your birthday could be the point when you evaluate the past year and set new goals. Thanksgiving is a great time to review the previous year in a positive light and be thankful.

Assess your relationships. Where is your marriage going? Are you growing more and more intimate or just coexisting? Is there a sense of purpose in your relationship? Take advantage of anniversaries to talk about where your relationship has been and where it's going. Write down your goals and review them later.

Set specific and general goals. In business, goals need to be concrete and measurable: selling fifteen million widgets in the Pacific Rim. That's not always necessary for personal and relationship goals. Still, it's helpful to put some numbers to your plans. "I want to spend five hours a week in quality conversation with my spouse." A great plan, but you don't need to take a stopwatch to the dinner table. Some goals need to be more general. "I want to be more creative at work." That's hard to measure, but at the end of the year you can recall several of your creative ideas and get a sense of your success. You need both kinds of goals to assess your life properly.

Include stretches and "softballs." Stretch yourself: "I will go to the gym three times a week." That's great, especially if your current gym membership involves only waving as you drive past it. But throw in a few "softballs"—easy-to-meet goals that will give you a sense of accomplishment. "I will start to write a novel." Starting is a great achievement, but it only takes a moment to do. Break down some big goals into smaller parts, so you can succeed, at least partially.

Pick a few points to work on. There are probably twenty ways you could improve your life in the next year. You'll get far more stressed if you tackle all twenty. Pick two or three to start with. As you meet a particular goal, pick another one.

Establish accountability. There are computer programs that can remind you of your goals and challenge you at regular intervals. Or you could ask your spouse. Perhaps you could team up with a friend at work, at church, or in the neighborhood. Whatever method you choose, we all do better when we have help staying on track. At the same time you might be accomplishing a relationship goal.

41. Are you able to assert your feelings in appropriate ways?

SOME PEOPLE ARE TEA KETTLES, BOILING AWAY IN SILENCE UNTIL they start screaming. Stress builds up within them and, if they don't express their feelings in healthy ways, they blow up, blasting everyone around them. If people don't communicate their feelings, they can cause themselves a host of physical problems, from indigestion to headaches to heart attacks. And when they finally erupt, they can damage their closest relationships.

These folks vacillate between two extremes. Often they're timid souls, accepting everything without a word. They feel embarrassed about complaining. Somewhere along the line they learned that nice people let others have their way. But each time they get hurt, they simmer a little more, until they finally boil over. Then they hit the other extreme, calling attention to their own needs and scorching everyone else.

They need to learn a middle way, a way of regular assertiveness. It's nice to be nice, but others need to know when they're hurting you. There's nothing wrong with telling others how you feel. In fact, it's an important way to vent your stress.

What to do?

Own your feelings; name your needs. Some people are so passive that they don't even admit to themselves when they feel hurt. You may need to talk yourself into a sense of assertiveness long before you communicate with anyone else. Understand that you have a lot to offer your community, your business, your family—but you need to be treated properly in order to function properly. You're not asking for special treatment—just reasonable, respectful treatment. You offer that to others; now you want some for yourself.

Pick an appropriate time and place to communicate. Once you've owned your feelings, you can begin to share them with others in your life. Design these encounters for the greatest chance of success. Think about when the other person will be most ready to hear what you have to say.

Couch your criticism in praise. If you have hard things to say, soften your comments by sincerely complimenting the other person first. You may want to start by saying how important the relationship is to you, and that's why you need to address this issue.

Speak the truth in love. Keep both of these in balance: honesty and kindness. Consider other people's feelings, but if you don't say the tough stuff, you're not being completely honest. If you criticize them in a nasty way, you're not being kind. Try to do both.

42. Do you place a high value on your primary relationship(s), and set aside time to work on improving it (them)?

A SUPPORTIVE RELATIONSHIP CAN CUSHION THE BLOWS OF life, empower you to face your daily challenges, and undergird you with a sense of security and significance.

We've talked about the stress that can come from our primary relationships. Even when they're good, they can create stress. But here we're talking about a reverse effect. Love can make life easier.

We're talking mainly about marriage. More than any other relationship, marriage has great potential to relieve the stress of life. Research shows that married people live longer. Why?

It gives you a sense of purpose. You're living your life for someone else now. You're needed. You're not depending entirely on your job for your significance.

It affirms you. In a supportive relationship, you're reminded that you are loved. You should also be complimented from time to time. No matter what anyone else in the world thinks of you, there's someone who thinks you're the greatest.

It brings you joy. Laughter is the best medicine for the stress of life, and a close relationship can give you that.

It offers distraction. In a loving home, you can retreat from the pressures of the workplace or the world.

It gives you a different perspective. You may be noodling some problem all day, then you mention it to your spouse and get the answer. Not that he or she is so brilliant; it's just that you need a new perspective.

It provides physical help and care. You can share the labor of your household. One person cooks and the other does the dishes. When one person is sick, the other can play nurse.

What to do?

Stop taking this relationship for granted. Make it a priority. Work at improving it. Understand that love is as important to your well-being as food.

Have fun. Sometimes books like this one talk so much about working on your relationships that you forget about enjoying them. The best relationships are those with laughter, with people who have fun together. Plan some happy activities.

Put it in your schedule. For many people, a marriage just fills the gaps in the schedule. If you're not doing anything else, you'll stay home. But then your schedule can fill up and you can become a stranger in your own home. Schedule times together to celebrate your relationship.

Read together. Go to a bookstore and pick out a marriage book that looks good to both of you. Then go through the chapters, pointing out things you think would be helpful to work on together.

Keep talking. Don't just talk about your relationship; talk about television shows you watch, movies you see, books you read. Talk about the events of your day. Discuss your hopes and dreams for the future.

Be a servant. Good marriages are built on mutual giving. Both partners need to seek the well-being of the other.

---

43. Do you have work, a hobby, or activities that give you a sense of meaning and purpose?

"I DON'T KNOW WHAT I'M GOOD FOR ANYMORE," THE MAN SAID. At seventy years of age, he was retired from his job and had felt rejected by a number of people he thought were his friends. Without anything to do, any way to make a difference, he was deeply depressed.

We talked a while about what he could do, what he had done in the past, and where he could find a place of service in his church or community. We suggested that he take some personality tests to determine his own skills and interests. He desperately needed a sense of meaning and purpose. When he felt the stress of personal rejection, he had nothing to fall back on.

Tom was in a similar situation years ago after his divorce. He didn't have much of a direction in life, so he had nothing to cushion his post-divorce stress. But he began hanging out with a friend who worked at a home for mentally retarded children. Tom was a mess, but these kids would flock around him, wanting to be his friends. What an encouragement! Since then he has often suggested that people volunteer to help needy children. It's about helping the kids, sure, but it also can give the helper a stronger sense of purpose in life.

You won't always find this sense of purpose on the job. It might come from a hobby, a community activity, a church involvement, or even a special relationship with someone in need.

What to do?

Learn what you can do. Take an aptitude test to determine your skills and interests. Or just make a list of the things you like to do. Consider activities you've had success with throughout your life, and things that you feel passionate about. Get some friends to brainstorm possibilities with you.

Look for meaning on the job. We know a receptionist in a medical office who hated the "busywork" of her job . . . until she realized that she was an important part of the healing process. "When people come into the office," she said, "they're hurting and afraid. They need to see a friendly face, someone who can help them, someone who can assure them they'll be all right." Maybe you too can find some greater purpose in an otherwise humdrum job.

Look elsewhere too. Sometimes you just have to let your job be just a job. It provides the money you need to live on while you do what you really love. Plenty of actors in New York and Los Angeles work as waiters. They find their significance in acting, and they do it whenever they can. They wait tables to pay the bills.

Volunteer. Still looking for meaningful activity? Volunteer for something. Many service organizations welcome volunteers. You may be stuffing envelopes or mopping floors at first—but for a good cause. And maybe they'll eventually see your talents and give you something more exciting to do.

Connect with others. Don't spend all your time alone with the model train set in your basement. Maybe that's your passion, but try to get out once in a while, at least to a model train convention. Share your activities with other people who have similar interests. That will help to affirm your sense of meaning.

44. Do you have a close network of friends or family to support you emotionally and spiritually?

PEOPLE ARE RELATIONAL BY NATURE. YES, THERE ARE SOME LON-ers around, but most of us need to connect with others at least some of the time. Most of the advantages we cited for primary relationships in question 42 also apply here to groups of family or friends. If you have a bunch of people around you who care about you, you'll be much better equipped to deal with stress.

You need:

Listeners. Sometimes you need to process your stress by talking it out. Good friends don't need to have all the answers. You just need to know someone cares.

Encouragers. When you're stressed, you need people to remind you that the future looks bright, that you can get through your problems, that you're on the right track. If you're doubting your own abilities, these friends can bolster your self-esteem.

Challengers. Sometimes you need friends to hold you accountable. If you're going in a bad direction, true friends will alert you to that and challenge you to get your act together. Sometimes it's hard to hear this stuff, but you need it.

Counselors. Often these are people who have gone through what you're going through. They have some wisdom to share with you. Of course, you may need to pull it out of them. The wisest friends aren't enamored with their own wisdom, but when you ask for advice, they'll give it.

Helpers. You also need friends who'll go beyond words and give you the concrete help you need. They'll give you a ride, get you a job, or baby-sit your kids so you and your mate can be alone. They're always looking for ways they can make your life better.

With friends like these, who needs stress? Seriously, your stress levels can be greatly reduced if you gather the right friends around you.

What to do?

Be a friend. As you deepen relationships with others, they'll be more apt to support you. Look around you for casual friendships that could become more important. Be there for people and they'll be there for you.

Find some elders. We normally find our friends among our peers, people of our own age and stage in life. But don't neglect your elders. They have a lot of wisdom to share.

Join a small group. Find a community or church group, perhaps gathered around a particular interest. This way you can make a number of friends at once.

Reach out. If you've moved to a new area, or if you're just slow to make friends, life can be pretty lonely. Don't wait for people to come to you. Get out there and circulate. Go to an evening school. Attend discussion groups in bookstores. Join a bowling league. Visit a church. With any of these activities, don't expect people to swamp you with friendship. You may feel like a stranger the first time or two. If you haven't made a friend by your third visit, start over somewhere else. In time, however, you should connect with someone who shares your interests.

PART NINE
Conclusion

IN this book, we've given you the tools to build a strategy for stress reduction. As we've shown, every person's stress is different. Your stress comes from different sources, and so there are several ways to reduce it—changing the stress factors in any of several environments, making sure you're healing properly from stress events, curbing your stress aggravators, or improving your stress fitness.

After reading the book, you may want to take the test again. Now that you know more about different stress-causing factors, you might answer some questions differently. Also, the stress events in your life keep changing, and that will change your entire stress profile. In fact, we recommend that you take the test every six months or so. That will help you keep up with your current stress events, and it will let you see your improvement as you work on various areas.

We wish you success as you address the stress issues in your life. Don't get all stressed out about stress reduction. Take one area at a time and try to make steady progress. Push yourself a little, but don't set your goals too high.

And let us know how you're doing. You can contact us (and get updated versions of the test) at our Web site, www.lifecounseling.org.

Now go to it!

NOTES

1. James E. Loehr, "Your Ideal Performance: A World-Class Trainer's System for Breaking Your Personal Achievement Records," *Success*, April 1997, p. 56.
2. *Success*, April 1997, p. 56.
3. Deborah Tannen, *Talking from 9 to 5* (New York: William Morrow & Co., 1994), p. 309.
4. Faith Popcorn and Lys Marigold, *Clicking* (New York: HarperCollins, 1996), p. 30.
5. Tom Whiteman and Randy Petersen, *Victim of Love?* (Colorado Springs, CO: Piñon Press, 1998), pp. 63-64.
6. Willard Harley, *His Needs, Her Needs* (Grand Rapids, MI: Revell, 1986), pp. 12-13.
7. Harley, p. 16.
8. G. K. Chesterton, "The Riddle of the Ivy," *The Man Who Was Chesterton* (New York: Image Books, 1960 [Dodd, Mead, 1937]), p. 64.
9 .Gary Chapman, *The Five Love Languages* (Chicago: Northfield, 1992).
10. Thomas A. Whiteman & Thomas G. Bartlett with Randy Petersen, *The Marriage Mender* (Colorado Springs, CO: NavPress, 1996), pp. 104-109.
11. Willard Harley, *Give & Take* (Grand Rapids, MI: Revell, 1996), p. 223.
12. Thomas A. Whiteman & Randy Petersen, *Becoming Your Own Best Friend* (Nashville, TN: Nelson, 1994), pp. 83-84.
13. Whiteman & Petersen, pp. 93-96.
14. Dietrich Bonhoeffer, *The Martyred Christian*, ed. by Joan Winmill Brown (New York: Collier, 1983), p. 153.
15. Anne Lamott, *Bird by Bird* (New York: Doubleday, 1994), p. 19.
16. Gurney Williams III, "Time-out: A surprising new cure for stress," *McCall's*, April 1997, p. 92.
17. Williams, p. 90.

AUTHORS

THOMAS WHITEMAN, Ph.D., is the founder and president of Life Counseling Services, a counseling center where he directs over fifty therapists, eight psychologists, and six psychiatrists. He is also president of Fresh Start Seminars, a nonprofit organization which conducts more than fifty divorce recovery seminars a year. Dr. Whiteman has authored or coauthored thirteen books.

He and his wife, Lori, have two daughters, Elizabeth and Michelle, and a son, Kurt. They live in Berwyn, Pennsylvania.

RANDY PETERSEN is a free-lance writer and is the author of more than twenty books, including several on psychological themes. He is coauthor of *The Complete Stress Management Workbook*. He is single and lives in Westville, New Jersey.

Healthy prescriptions for stress from Dr. Richard Swenson.

Margin

Are you worn out? This book offers healthy living in four areas
we all struggle with—emotional energy, physical energy, time, and
finances—and will prepare you to live a balanced life.
Margin $12

The Overload Syndrome

Feeling overwhelmed? Examine the nature of this common
problem and learn practical tools for managing overload in the
most foundational areas of your life.
The Overload Syndrome $12

Get your copies today at your local bookstore, through our
website, or by calling (800) 366-7788. Ask for offer **#6004** or a
FREE catalog of NavPress resources.

NAVPRESS
BRINGING TRUTH TO LIFE
www.navpress.com

Prices subject to change.